W9-AQR-756

DATE DUE

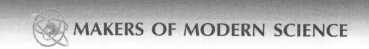
MAKERS OF MODERN SCIENCE

Barbara McClintock

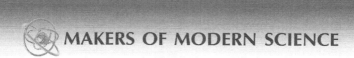

MAKERS OF MODERN SCIENCE

Barbara McClintock

Pioneering Geneticist

RAY SPANGENBURG AND DIANE KIT MOSER

CHELSEA HOUSE
PUBLISHERS
An imprint of Infobase Publishing

Barbara McClintock: Pioneering Geneticist

Copyright © 2008 by Ray Spangenburg and Diane Kit Moser

Chelsea House
An imprint of Infobase Publishing
132 West 31st Street
New York NY 10001

ISBN-10: 0-8160-6172-6
ISBN-13: 978-0-8160-6172-3

Library of Congress Cataloging-in-Publication Data

Spangenburg, Ray, 1939–
    Barbara McClintock: pioneering geneticist / Ray Spangenburg and
    Diane Kit Moser
        p. cm.—(Makers of modern science)
    Includes bibliographical references and index.
    ISBN 0-8160-6172-6
    1. McClintock, Barbara, 1902–1992—Juvenile literature. 2. Geneticists—United States—Biography—Juvenile literature. I. Moser, Diane, 1944– . II. Title.
QH429.2.M38S63 2007
576.5092—dc22   2006032356

Chelsea House books are available at special discounts when purchased in bulk quantities for businesses, associations, institutions, or sales promotions. Please call our Special Sales Department in New York at (212) 967-8800 or (800) 322-8755.

You can find Chelsea House on the World Wide Web at
http://www.chelseahouse.com

Text design and composition by Kerry Casey
Cover design by Salvatore Luongo
Illustrations by Chris and Elisa Scherer
Cover printed by Maple Press, York, PA
Book printed and bound by Maple Press, York, PA
Date printed: September, 2010
Printed in the United States of America

10 9 8 7 6 5 4 3 2

This book is printed on acid-free paper.

For all scientists, both sung and unsung,
who, in the words of Carl Sagan,
have spent their lives lighting
"candles in the dark"

CONTENTS

PREFACE

....

Science is, above all, a great human adventure. It is the process of exploring what Albert Einstein called the "magnificent structure" of nature using observation, experience, and logic. Science comprises the best methods known to humankind for finding reliable answers about the unknown. With these tools, scientists probe the great mysteries of the universe—from black holes and star nurseries to deep-sea hydrothermal vents (and extremophile organisms that survive high temperatures to live in them); from faraway galaxies to subatomic particles such as quarks and antiquarks; from signs of life on other worlds to microorganisms such as bacteria and viruses here on Earth; from how a vaccine works to protect a child from disease to the DNA, genes, and enzymes that control traits and processes from the color of a boy's hair to how he metabolizes sugar.

Some people think that science is rigid and static, a dusty, musty set of facts and statistics to memorize for a test and then forget. Some think of science as antihuman—devoid of poetry, art, and a sense of mystery. Yet science is based on a sense of wonder and is all about exploring the mysteries of life and our planet and the vastness of the universe. Science offers methods for testing and reasoning that help keep us honest with ourselves. As physicist Richard Feynman once said, science is above all a way to keep from fooling yourself—or letting nature (or others) fool you. Nothing could be more growth-oriented or more human. Science evolves continually. New bits of knowledge and fresh discoveries endlessly shed new light and offer new perspectives. As a result, science is constantly undergoing revolutions—ever refocusing what scientists have explored before into fresh, new understanding. Scientists like to say science is self-correcting. That is, science is fallible, and scientists can be wrong. It is easy to fool yourself, and it is easy to be fooled by others, but because new facts are constantly flowing in, scientists are continually refining their work to account for as many facts as possible. So science can make mistakes, but it also auto-corrects.

Sometimes, as medical scientist Jonas Salk liked to point out, good science thrives when scientists ask the right question about what they observe. "What people think of as the moment of discovery is really the discovery of the question," he once remarked.

There is no one, step-by-step "scientific method" that all scientists use. However, science requires the use of methods that are systematic, logical, and *empirical* (based on objective observation and experience). The goal of science is to explore and understand how nature works—what causes the patterns we see or experience, the shapes we find, the colors, the textures, the consistency, the mass, all the characteristics of the natural universe.

What is it like to be a scientist and actually do science? Many people think of television and movie stereotypes when they think of scientists—the cartoonlike view of the "mad" scientist or the scientist entrapped in excesses of "cold logic." In general, though, these portrayals represent more imagination than truth. Scientists know how to use their brains. They are exceptionally good with the tools of logic and critical thinking. However, that is about where the generalizations stop being accurate. Although science follows strict rules, it is often guided by the many styles and personalities of the scientists themselves, the people who *do* science—and the many faces of science also have distinct individuality, personality, and style. What better way to explore what science is all about than through the experiences of great scientists?

Each volume of the Makers of Modern Science set presents the life and life work of a prominent scientist whose outstanding contributions in his or her field have garnered the respect and recognition of other prominent colleagues. These profiled men and women were all great scientists, but they differed in many ways. Their approaches to the use of science were different: Niels Bohr was a theoretical physicist whose strengths lay in patterns, ideas, and conceptualization, while Wernher von Braun was a hands-on scientist/engineer who led the team that built the giant rocket used by Apollo astronauts to reach the Moon. Some had genius sparked by solitary contemplation: Geneticist Barbara McClintock worked alone in fields of maize and sometimes spoke to no one all day long. Others worked as members of large, coordinated teams. Oceanographer Robert Ballard organized oceangoing ship crews on submersible expeditions to the ocean floor; biologist Jonas Salk established the Salk Institute to help scientists in different fields collaborate more freely and study the human body through the interrelationships of their differing knowledge and approaches. Their personal styles also differed: Biologist Rita Levi-Montalcini enjoyed wearing chic dresses and makeup; McClintock was sunburned and wore baggy denim jeans and an oversize shirt; nuclear physicist Richard Feynman was a practical joker and an energetic bongo drummer.

The chosen scientists represent a spectrum of disciplines and a diversity of approaches to science as well as lifestyles. Each biography explores the scientist's younger years along with his or her education and growth as a scientist; the experiences, research, and contributions of the maturing scientist; and the course of the path to recognition. Each volume also explores the nature of science and its unique usefulness for studying the universe, as well as sidebars covering related facts or profiles of interest, introductory coverage of the scientist's field, line illustrations and photographs, a timeline, a glossary of related scientific terms, and a list of further resources including books, Web sites, periodicals, and associations.

The volumes in the Makers of Modern Science set offer a factual look at the lives and exciting contributions of the profiled scientists—in the hope that readers will see science as a uniquely human quest to understand the universe and that some readers may be inspired as well to follow in the footsteps of these great scientists.

ACKNOWLEDGMENTS

The authors wish to express appreciation to the many individuals who helped with this book, either directly or indirectly, including archivists Clare Clark of Cold Spring Harbor Laboratory Archives, Kathy Wyss of Indiana University, Kristopher Anstine at the University of Missouri, Linda Bustos at Caltech, as well as Barbara McClintock's niece, Marjorie M. Bhavnani. Additionally, we wish to thank our visionary and hard-working editor, Frank K. Darmstadt, for his patience and belief in us, and our good friend and agent, Linda Allen.

Finally, special thanks to Lee B. Kass, Ph.D., a science history scholar and researcher who has extensively written about and researched McClintock's career for her forthcoming intellectual biography of McClintock. A visiting professor of botany in the Plant Biology Department at Cornell University, where McClintock both studied and taught, Lee Kass has read and reread our manuscript and made countless valuable and insightful suggestions, thereby saving us from many gaffes. She was tireless in her pursuit of objectivity and generous with her time, her help, and her knowledge and understanding of the subject. Any mistakes or missteps that remain, of course, are purely our own.

INTRODUCTION

This volume of the Makers of Modern Science set profiles geneticist Barbara McClintock, whose 70 years of meticulously conceived and executed experiments in the genetics of maize, or Indian corn, have increasingly become recognized for their contributions to today's most cutting-edge technology and science, including genetic engineering and bacterial reactions to antibiotics.

McClintock's deep commitment and determination combined with the fascinating intricacies and challenges of her chosen field to produce a dramatic story of discovery and achievement—despite a social milieu that did not embrace science as a "woman's career." McClintock made her own rules and explored the frontiers as she chose them at a time when these characteristics were not usually appreciated in women.

At the dawn of the 20th century when Barbara McClintock was born, the scientific arena of genetics was a new, little-known territory, and the words *gene* and *genetics* had not yet been coined. Scientific research showed clearly the connection between genes and inheritance, but scientists were still left wondering how so few genes control so many different traits for the myriad types of tissues in an organism. No one yet had even dreamed of the complex intricacies of structure and function inherent in DNA, or imagined its existence. By the time McClintock was 19, she was poised at the perfect moment to become a pioneer in the field of genetics. Like the maize plants she cultivated and studied, the science of genetics grew in and around her life. She quickly earned the respect of her peers as a razor-sharp, independent thinker. Genetics would become McClintock's life work, a work that, once started, would shape her days for the rest of her life. The 20th century turned out to be the century of the gene, with explosions of discovery illuminating its

days and today, McClintock's key discovery—known as the "jumping gene"—forms the cornerstone of much of genetic engineering, one of the great fields of growth of our time.

At Cornell University, where McClintock studied and began her research, she enjoyed early recognition for her brilliant mind, meticulously designed experiments, intense focus, and carefully observed results. Later she received numerous mid-career honors, including election to membership at 41 to the National Academy of Sciences and election the following year to the presidency of the Genetics Society of America. Suddenly, however, the pace of her career seemed to slow visibly after she presented a set of radical-sounding results at the 1951 symposium held at Cold Spring Harbor Laboratory, where she was assured a lifetime position as a research scientist. The reception was unenthusiastic—many or most of those attending considered her conclusions too far out of step with current theories. Had the rest of genetics passed McClintock by while she labored in her cornfields?

McClintock was disappointed, and after awhile she stopped publishing, except for her contributions to the Cold Spring Harbor annual report. But she did not give up, continuing to amass data in support of her conclusions and receiving continued support from Cold Spring Harbor for her research. As it turned out, McClintock's work would wait 20 years for geneticists to recognize its importance and more than 30 years for real validation. It was a long wait, but McClintock knew her research was sound and never let the lack of encouragement and recognition stop her. She loved her work and knew her own value.

When recognition came, it arrived in the form of the most prestigious award in science: the Nobel Prize. In 1983, Barbara McClintock became the first woman to become the sole recipient of the Nobel Prize in physiology or medicine. The question that immediately comes to mind is "Why?" Why did recognition of McClintock's contribution come so many decades after that first presentation in 1951? Thirty years later, in 1981, *Time* magazine pronounced her a "modern Mendel," and the comparison is apt in many ways. Like the 19th-century monk Gregor Mendel,

McClintock was a plant geneticist whose results came from years of carefully controlled generations of plants. Like him, she toiled alone, conceiving her experiments and completing their requirements with careful ritual, often in nearly monastic silence. Coincidentally, like Mendel's work, hers went unnoticed until other aspects of genetic research fell into place, like pieces in a jigsaw puzzle, so other scientists could see where her observations fit. By the time Francis Crick and James Watson established the structure of DNA in 1953, and Marshall W. Nirenberg, Robert W. Holley, and Gobind Khorana showed how DNA determines the structure of proteins, Barbara McClintock's contention that mobile elements existed in genes began to look much less questionable. By the time other scientists identified mobile genetic elements in other organisms, the case became conclusive.

Barbara McClintock was above all consistent with her inner nature, living a simple, unencumbered life designed to fulfill her longing for knowledge. Her entire life revolved around her intensely focused pursuit of natural science. People thought she was saintly or heroic or eccentric, but in fact, she was the individual she set out to be as a child, an individual who "loved knowing things." In that sense, she was a role model—not necessarily for her lifestyle or even her management of adversity, but for the way she listened to her inner self.

People have often pointed to McClintock's story as a tale of neglect and bias against a woman-scientist, and unquestionably, the sciences were among the last bastions of a world that tended to sideline even brilliant women such as McClintock into adjunct and inferior positions, rarely allowing potentials to develop. Along with her female colleagues, McClintock did experience discrimination, but she earned and received the respect of her male peers. She was one of the strong, determined, capable women who broke through barriers and ceilings and helped make careers in science a ready option for the young women attending universities today.

At the same time, McClintock had personal characteristics that both helped and hindered her. College administrators often saw her as "troublesome" and "difficult." She was a loner who prided herself on her ability to take care of every aspect of an experiment—planting the corn kernels, cultivating and watering, pollinating, collecting kernels and labeling them, preparing microscope slides, and interpreting the results. She found joy in it all. But, like Mendel, she became isolated because she spent so much time alone.

This book tells the story of Barbara McClintock and her pursuit of *cytogenetics,* the study of cell structure and function by exploring how elements within a cell relate to inherited traits. Her story is inseparable from the exciting discovery of what the media called "jumping genes," or mobile gene elements. It embraces her unflinching pursuit of her results despite the unpopularity of her analysis. It explores both her sense of inadequacy, from which her creative productivity emerged, and her self-assurance. It is the story of her life, the joy she found in her work, the pain she experienced at its initial rejection, and the contributions she made to understanding how genes work.

It is also a saga that illustrates the fine line between success and failure. For Barbara McClintock, what really mattered was the work itself and the satisfaction she enjoyed in her daily life. She cared intensely about what she was doing, and that intensity and commitment, in the end, was what mattered to her above all else.

What was Barbara McClintock really like and how did she use aspects of her own character to enable her work? Those who knew her best recognized that she had a towering ego—she knew she was brilliant, yet was also sensitive and needful of protection and intellectual stimulation. She was an enthusiastic storyteller and she developed an arsenal of stories—sometimes called "myths" or a "public persona" by recent biographers and researchers. She evidently used this facade to project a carefully controlled image of herself. Casting aside trendy psychological terms, this book for the first time explores these ideas for the teen audience, recognizing that most people create a self-image they project at least to some extent, as McClintock did. McClintock gave interviews in the last 10 to 15 years of her life that recalled events as she remembered them, painted with the patina of time. Recent research has shown that some stories could not have happened as she recollected them. She simplified here, amplified there, and molded memories to fit her self-image; it was a natural and not necessarily deliberate process. This book retells many of her stories but puts them in context and recounts them as part of an artfully drawn life, which she enthusiastically would tell the world was "a very, very satisfying and interesting life." That was her underlying premise, and no one, surely, could question the truth of that.

Born to Seek Knowledge

(1902–1918)

When Barbara McClintock was born on June 16, 1902, in Hartford, Connecticut, the scientific study of genetics was also in its infancy—but it was a field destined to burst upon the century's consciousness in a remarkable series of explosions. In that same year, British biologist William Bateson wrote that "an exact determination of the laws of heredity will probably work more change in man's outlook on the world, and in his power over nature, than any other advance in natural knowledge that can be clearly foreseen." The remarkable accuracy of this forecast would probably have surprised even Bateson, speaking as he was at the very beginning of a period that has become known in biology as the "century of the gene."

Barbara McClintock brought incredible gifts to the development of the science of genetics—keen curiosity, tireless experimentation and attention to detail, flawless laboratory technique,

1

uncommonly lucid overarching comprehension, and, most important of all, the ability to integrate her observations into meaningful insights. Unquestionably, she was in many ways the right combination of skill and intelligence in the right place at the right time, ready to jump into action just under two decades later.

Eleanor McClintock (who was renamed Barbara) was the third of four children born to Sara Handy McClintock and Thomas Henry McClintock. She had two older sisters, Marjorie (born in 1898) and Mignon (born in 1900), and a brother, Malcolm Rider (born in 1903), informally known as Tom.

Descendants of the Mayflower in her mother's family took pride in lineage, social standing, and wealth as standards of success, but Sara Handy was an independent thinker whose favorite quote came from her unconventional, seafaring grandfather, who liked to say, "Don't it beat all how people act if you don't think their way?" Against her father's will, Sara married Tom McClintock, a penniless medical student at the time. The two combined their funds to start up his medical practice.

Having received a conventional education for young women of her time and background, Sara wrote poetry, painted, and played the piano skillfully, and she bolstered the family income by taking in piano students. As a young woman, Sara Handy McClintock was unimpressed with lineage; she was strong-minded and insistent on self-reliance, self-determination, and independence—traits that would soon reappear, much stronger, in her daughter Barbara.

An Appreciation for Solitude

By the time Barbara was born, her mother had the usual problems of a working parent—too little time, too much work, and too much fatigue—and an adversarial relationship developed between them. Barbara much preferred to be left alone. Her mother later recounted how Barbara would hide among the window curtains and scream, "Don't touch me! Don't touch me!"

Barbara's parents sent her to stay with an aunt (her father's sister) and uncle, and McClintock later asserted that she preferred living there, away from her family. Her uncle was a fish seller, a practical, outgoing man who took her along on his neighborhood rounds selling and delivering fish. In those intermittent stays with her relatives, Barbara may have developed the beginnings of her hearty love of the outdoors.

In 1908, the year Barbara turned six, her family settled in Brooklyn, New York. During the years in Brooklyn, Tom McClintock's practice became more successful, and the family began to spend summers in the countryside around nearby Long Beach. There Barbara enjoyed walking alone along the beach or running with a dog at her side. She especially liked running at an effortless, straight-backed, floating stride she had discovered and found exhilarating. This practice engaged a sort of freedom from self, a Zen-like exercise that she frequently used in later life to enhance her focus on a problem to be solved.

Barbara continued to seek out solitary activities—reading or just sitting, deeply immersed in her own thoughts. Her family learned to accept her need for space and solitude. "Barbs was simply Barbs," her sister Marjorie explained decades later in an interview with science historian Evelyn Fox Keller. Barbara, her family had realized, was different.

As she grew up, the McClintocks began to understand and respect Barbara's commitment to freedom and independence, which remained a key to her success throughout her life. When Barbara developed a love for ice-skating, her parents not only bought her the best pair of ice-skates they could find but also defended her decision

Barbara McClintock and her siblings (left to right): Mignon, Malcolm Rider (Tom), Barbara, and Marjorie, ca. 1907 (Marjorie M. Bhavnani, through the American Philosophical Society)

to skip school to practice ice-skating. Her mother also took her side against a nosy neighbor who criticized Barbara for wearing pants and playing team sports with the neighborhood boys.

McClintock did not recall having any childhood friends who were girls. She explained to Keller, "I didn't play with girls because they didn't play the way I did. I liked athletics, ice skating, roller skating, and bicycling, just to throw a ball and enjoy the rhythm of pitch and catch; it has a very wonderful rhythm." However, even though Barbara's teammates had considered her part of the team in their practice sessions, her teammates became embarrassed when she came along to an away game and would not let her play because she was a girl. As it turned out, the other team was one player short and let her play on their side. She played, helping them beat her own team, and, as a result, she got called a traitor all the way home. As McClintock put it later, "So you couldn't win. You had to be alone."

As a child growing up, McClintock came to think of herself as a maverick, independent and intellectually original. She was proud of her self-reliance and thought of herself as a free spirit. Whether genetics or her environment influenced the future scientist's character more, no one will probably ever know, but her mother's stories certainly reinforced Barbara's image of herself as a renegade. Her mother painted a picture of a remarkable baby, happy to sit on a pillow playing alone for hours. From her earliest childhood, McClintock remembered having an affinity for solitude. This remarkable trait would become a key to her way of life, her life work, and her approach to thinking and solving problems. As a girl growing up and later in her life as a scientist, Barbara McClintock used her solitary time to focus single-mindedly on her projects.

Once Barbara reached puberty, however, her mother, who had defended her activities before, now suddenly expected her to set aside what she considered Barbara's frolicking childhood amusements to become a young woman. In her mother's eyes, the time had come for Barbara to take up the serious business of finding a man who would marry and support her.

Thirst for Knowledge

Barbara, as usual, had a different focus. At Erasmus Hall High School in Brooklyn, she did fall in love—not with the eligible young man her mother envisioned, but with knowledge. "I loved information," she explained years later in an interview with Keller. "I loved to know things."

During her years at Erasmus, she developed a fascination for science. Problem solving, to her, became "just pure joy." She often solved classroom exercises in unusual ways and liked to conceive several different ways to arrive at answers. For Barbara McClintock, this period in her life shaped her future as a ceaselessly probing, curious individual who loved intellectual challenges and relentlessly sought out answers. Later she would develop an intuitive sense of priority and could zero in on the key problems in her field, but she began with keen curiosity and innate problem-solving skill, both of which received encouragement from her teachers at Erasmus.

Brooklyn and Erasmus Hall High School

When the McClintocks moved to Brooklyn in 1908, the Brooklyn Bridge had already connected the eastern borough to Manhattan for 25 years. The area's population was growing rapidly, but many neighborhoods retained a pleasant, semirural character well into the 1940s, sprinkled with truck farms maintained by local Italian-American farmers.

Erasmus Hall High School, where Barbara McClintock and her sisters and brother attended school, was founded in 1787 as a small private academy with only 26 students. Located at the corner of Flatbush and Church Avenues, it is known today as the "mother of high schools" as a tribute to its history as the first secondary school to be chartered by New York State and the flagship school of the state's public school system. Clearly an environment that nourishes imagination and creativity, the school has produced an astonishing mix of famous and talented graduates, among them actors Jeff Chandler, Susan Hayward, Barbara Stanwyck, Eli Wallach, and Mae West; singers Barbra Streisand, James D-Train Williams, and Beverly Sills; chess champion Bobby Fischer; authors Bernard Malamud, Robert Silverberg, and Mickey Spillane; and, of course, geneticist Barbara McClintock.

College: To Go or Not to Go?

During the years that Barbara attended high school, World War I had temporarily removed her father from the McClintock family's daily life. A member of the National Guard, he was called up and sent to serve in Europe as a military surgeon. During these same years, Barbara and her sisters were becoming young women. Both Marjorie and Mignon were excellent students, and Marjorie received a scholarship offer to attend Vassar College, a prestigious (and expensive) college for women. Sara McClintock was concerned about financial costs as well as what she saw as social disadvantages of higher education for women. She believed that a college degree made a young woman seem more intellectual and less marriageable, and she dissuaded both older daughters from going on to college. With their mother making the decision in her husband's absence, both acquiesced, and Marjorie gave up her scholarship.

Barbara did not give in so easily. She was determined to pursue the knowledge she had come to love, and as her mother had also done as a young woman, she listened to her own priorities. Her mother remained firm, fearing that a college education would make her daughter "a strange person, a person who didn't belong to society." Worst of all, in Sara McClintock's view, perhaps she would become a college professor. At the time, women could not even vote in the United States, and a young woman's future typically depended on the talents and socioeconomic standing of her future husband.

In an interview with Keller, McClintock later recalled refusing to give up: "I would take the consequences for the sake of an activity that I knew would give me great pleasure. And I would do that regardless of the pain—not flaunting it, but as a decision that it was the only way that I could keep my sanity, to follow that kind of regime."

Faced with a shortage of funds, though, she realized her prospects for college were growing dim. After graduation from high school, she took a job working for an unemployment agency and spent evenings studying in the library. The summer nights passed quickly, and the fall term loomed ahead. Then the war ended and her father returned from France. Initially, he agreed with his wife's judgment, but Barbara had always been special in his mind. As McClintock later recounted

The McClintock family (left to right): Marjorie, Malcolm Rider (Tom), Barbara, Mignon, and mother Sara at the piano, ca. 1918 (Marjorie M. Bhavnani, through the American Philosophical Society)

to Keller, "My father was an M.D. though. He sensed from the beginning that I would be going into graduate work. He didn't want me to be an M.D. He thought I would be treated so badly. Women got such nasty treatment. But he warned me; he didn't coerce me. He was supportive with me. He had great faith I'd come out all right." And so his youngest daughter succeeded in persuading him to see her side. She would go to college.

Science as a Way
of Finding Out

(1919–1927)

T he decision was firm. Now Sara McClintock shifted gears and swung into action to make her daughter's vision of a college education become a reality. They quickly settled on Cornell University, which was tuition-free for residents of New York State. Relieved of the responsibility for making the final decision, Sara quickly became as great a supporter of Barbara's future as she previously had been an objector. It was already late summer, and registration was set to begin the following week. So, McClintock recalled 60 years later, students with last names beginning with M were due to enroll on Tuesday, so Sara checked with Erasmus Hall High School and made travel arrangements. Barbara arrived at Cornell in the upstate New York town of Ithaca on Monday and found a rooming house that would become home for the school year. On Tuesday, she was standing in line early for registration,

when a large obstacle appeared before her in the person of the registrar himself.

Where were her papers? he boomed. Unruffled, McClintock
explained that she knew nothing about that; she was there to reg-

☀ Women in Science

In the decades leading up to 1919, relatively few young women
sought a college education, and of those who did, few gained admit-
tance. Once graduated, fewer still would obtain career positions
that acknowledged their education and capabilities. The inequality
was even greater in Europe, where just a few years earlier a woman
could consider herself fortunate to be allowed to audit classes (that
is, attend a class without receiving credits). Once she had demon-
strated considerable ability, she might be "allowed," as happened to
mathematician Amalie (Emmy) Noether in Germany, to teach a class
without pay. Yet finally in 1904, the University of Erlangen lifted the
rule against women enrolling, and in 1908, Noether received her
doctorate summa cum laude (with highest honors).

By contrast, the United States seemed at least a little more
progressive. In the late 19th and early 20th centuries, several private
colleges for women, some affiliated with all-male colleges such as
Harvard, offered accredited higher education for women—and had
women on their faculty. In addition, at least two colleges existed that
allowed enrollment to women alongside men: Oberlin College in Ohio
and Barbara McClintock's choice, Cornell University in Ithaca, New
York. During these years, several women of high distinction emerged
to find challenging careers in science, receiving recognition for their
work—not recognition equivalent to men, but recognition. In particular, the names of Maria Mitchell, Annie Jump Cannon, and Henrietta
Swan Leavitt come to mind (all, as it happened, in astronomy).

Maria Mitchell did not attend a college or university, having
learned astronomy from her father, but after discovering a comet
in 1847, she received honors usually reserved for men at the time,
including election to the American Academy of Arts and Sciences
(the first woman to receive that honor), the American Association for
the Advancement of Science, and the American Philosophical Society.
She also served for many years as professor of astronomy at Vassar.

Annie Jump Cannon graduated from Wellesley College (a private
college for women) in 1884, following up with coursework at Welles-

ister. How did she expect to register without papers? McClintock never flinched, and at that moment (so the story goes), a stack of papers arrived and, as if by magic, hers were among them. The registrar waved her on, and she was in!

ley and Radcliffe (a private college for women, affiliated with Harvard, where Radcliffe students sometimes enrolled in courses). Cannon joined the mostly male staff of Harvard College Observatory in 1896, becoming curator of astronomical photographs in 1911. She is best known for her contributions to a catalog of more than 350,000 stellar spectra, but she also discovered some 300 variable stars and five novas and is widely respected as a great astronomer.

Henrietta Swan Leavitt attended Oberlin College in Ohio and graduated from Radcliffe (known at the time as the Society for the Educational Instruction of Women). Like Cannon, Leavitt worked at Harvard Observatory, volunteering in 1895 and later receiving payment at 30 cents an hour. There she discovered 1,777 new variable stars, but more important was her key discovery in 1912 known as the Cepheid variable period-luminosity relationship. This discovery greatly improved the accuracy of measurement of distances outside our galaxy—a major contribution. Unfortunately, she did not receive the freedom from her employer at the observatory to follow up on her discovery.

Henrietta Leavitt (1868–1921) discovered a method for measuring the size of the universe. (Margaret Harwood, AIP Emilio Segrè Visual Archives, Shapley Collection)

The story of McClintock's registration day at Cornell contributed to her self-confessed lifelong belief that she was naturally "lucky." She did not question why or how her paperwork turned up in just the right place and time. Barbara's sister Marjorie once suggested that this was another example of the energetic efforts of Sara McClintock, operating behind the scenes. Whatever the explanation, Barbara was unsurprised. She simply accepted this highly satisfactory outcome and carried on, eagerly exploring the path that had opened up before her. Maybe this reaction helped her both minimize her personal importance—a lifelong practice—and at the same time justify in her mind why she was the only one of her siblings to go to college. In any case, as irrational as the idea of her luck may have been, McClintock clung to it.

College Days at Cornell University (1919–1923)

Regarding higher education for women, Barbara McClintock found Cornell University was ahead of its time in several ways. Founded in 1865 by Ezra Cornell and Andrew Dickson White as a private institution of higher learning, Cornell touted as its motto these broadly democratic sentiments, framed in the words of banker/founder Ezra Cornell: "I would found an institution where any person can find instruction in any study." Applicants were welcomed regardless of gender, nationality, race, social status, or religion.

The university also was (and is) the federal land-grant institution for the state of New York. That meant that while offering the richness of a classical Ivy League education, Cornell was also required to offer tuition-free courses in state-supported divisions, including the College of Agriculture (an umbrella that covered life sciences as well as home economics). McClintock had chosen well, both educationally and economically: As a student in the College of Agriculture, she was entitled to a tuition-free education, including every class that was available to any other student at Cornell.

McClintock's presence as a woman in the higher education system was not as unusual in the 1920s as it had been in previous decades. Surprisingly, of all graduate students in the United States in the 1920s, some 30 to 40 percent were women. About 12 percent of the doctorates in science and engineering were women—higher than any period before or since, until the 1970s. In the sciences, most women nationwide favored biology, and of those, many opted for botany, with many attracted to genetics. However, once a woman acquired a good science education, almost no future existed for these women of science, aside from teaching science at a women's college, with little opportunity for research appointments. Jobs in research—whether in universities, colleges, private enterprise, or government—were almost all reserved exclusively for men. This ubiquitous roadblock made McClintock's achievements all the more stunning.

McClintock's life at Cornell was everything she had hoped it would be. She lost herself in the life of the mind, entranced by the intellectual thrill of embracing new ideas, solving problems, and soaking up knowledge.

McClintock began to have a social life too, making friends, as she later recalled, with a group of women students who gathered in a large corner suite in an on-campus dormitory. One of the few members of the group who was not Jewish and the only scientist, she enjoyed the sharp witticisms and intellectual tone of their discussions. She also liked being part of a group that was so "different from the rest of the population at Cornell," as she would later put it, and she learned to read Yiddish out of an interest in their culture.

Popular and outgoing, at the end of her first year, McClintock was elected president of women freshman students. Just over five feet tall, slender, and wiry, she had a strong personality, enjoyed a good joke, and had a hearty, uninhibited laugh.

Also during her first year, she pledged and joined a sorority but soon felt extreme discomfort with the division emphasized by sororities between those who were "in" and those who were "out." Concluding her experiment with the social mainstream, McClintock backed out of her pledge and remained uncomfortable for the rest of her life with the privileges and accolades that came with honorary awards and election to various professional societies. In thinking back on her sorority experience, she later remarked to Keller, "Many of these girls were very nice girls, but I was immediately aware that there were those who made it and those who didn't. Here was a dividing line that put you in one category or the other. And I couldn't take it. So I thought about it for a while, and broke my pledge. . . . I just couldn't stand that kind of discrimination. It was so shocking that I never really got over it . . ."

McClintock is believed to have lived alone most of her life and she liked to point out, as she did to Evelyn Keller, that she never felt the need for day-to-day live-in companionship. She said that as a student at Cornell she dated frequently, especially during the first two years, but she later recalled these relationships as an "emotional attachment, nothing else."

"These attachments wouldn't have lasted," she stressed in an interview with Evelyn Fox Keller. McClintock recognized that she was not constructed to fit into someone else's life. "There was not that strong necessity for a personal attachment to anybody," she continued. "I just didn't feel it. And I could never understand marriage. I really do not even now. . . . I never went through the experience of requiring it."

McClintock was not wrapped up with the process of succeeding at a career in science. Not driven by ego, she functioned best and was happiest when she was outside "the me"—as she was as a child running, almost floating above the sand on the beach. She had had a taste during her childhood of operating outside herself, as an objective observer. This was her ultimate pleasure in science and gift to science, and she was happiest when she was able to lose herself in her work. For her, the joy was always in finding the answer to a puzzle, combining the creativity of her genius with the rigor of scientific method, and leaving no ends loose.

One by one, McClintock began to reset her priorities and eliminate conflicts. During much of her undergraduate career, she played tenor banjo in a jazz combo. Like many students of math and science, she was attracted to music theory and its mathematical structure, and she had a natural talent for playing. She and a group of friends played gigs frequently at local cafés and other venues down the hill from Cornell in the town of Ithaca. (In fact, getting down the steep hill was often a challenge, especially in the icy months of winter. McClintock liked to tell the story of a time when she just gave up walking down the hill and sat down on the ice and slid to the bottom.) As her student years passed and her studies in science intensified, she found that the demands of her coursework began to take up so much of her time that one evening during a gig she felt a sudden jolt in the midst of playing a piece. She was convinced she had dropped off to sleep in the middle of a performance and, although her fellow players insisted all was well, she decided the time had come to hang up her banjo for good.

McClintock was in the process of shaping a unique lifestyle defined by its focus on her scientific work. Earlier, in her first year, she had decided her long hair only got in her way—and she had a barber cut her hair short. Within a couple of years, "bobbed" (short) hair became widely popular among young women of her generation, but in 1919 and 1920, it was still a startlingly radical hairstyle. McClintock's practical mind-set ruled again when she chose her clothing for working in the experimental fields as a graduate student. On the premise that skirts and dresses would only snag on plants and pose problems, she settled on knickers (knee-length pants like golf pants). Again, a sensible but radical choice for her time.

This reshaping of McClintock's personal life began to take firm hold in her junior year, when she took her first course in genetics. Her interest was so intense and her promise so clear that she was invited to follow up with graduate courses and seminars that were usually reserved for more advanced students. As McClintock later wrote, "When the undergraduate genetics course was completed in January 1922, I received a telephone call from Dr. [C. B.] Hutchison [who taught the course]. He must have sensed my intense interest in the content of his course because the purpose of his call was to invite me to participate in the only other genetics course given at Cornell. It was scheduled for graduate students. His invitation was accepted with pleasure and great anticipations. Obviously, this telephone call cast the die for my future. I remained with genetics thereafter."

McClintock completed her bachelor's degree from Cornell in 1923. By then she was truly hooked on science, attracted by the scientific approach and its methodical path to knowledge in a natural universe that is full of questions. Genetics was fast becoming a hot topic (as it still is), and McClintock was drawn to the exciting discoveries being made.

Genetics: The Story So Far

By the time Barbara McClintock began her studies at Cornell, farmers, ranchers, and naturalists had been studying inherited characteristics in animals and plants for centuries, even millennia. People usually had a job in mind for the animals they bred, and they were eager to encourage useful traits (such as resistance to disease) and suppress traits they saw as negative (such as vulnerability to disease). Breeders were eager to discover how traits are passed from generation to generation. The same was true of plants raised as food, medicine, decoration, and other uses. However, no one had pushed these questions further to get at what the agents and processes were—not, that is, until a lone Augustinian monk named Gregor Mendel entered the scene in the latter half of the 19th century.

Gardening as Science

Mendel thought of his project more as a gardening hobby than a grand experiment in heredity, but he pursued it with the same passion for detail and experiment that any other scientist would. He brought to his experiments an unusual combination of talents in plant breeding and mathematics—an approach no one else had discussed in previous publications. So it was that he embarked upon an amazing project, one that absorbed tremendous energy for years, for the same reason that most scientists "do science": unyielding curiosity.

Soon after entering the monastery, Mendel began trying to breed different colors in flowers. This kind of enterprise was not unusual; controlling flower colors and enhancing their beauty had lured plant breeders for centuries. Along the way, Mendel acquired experience in the process of artificial fertilization in plants, and he noticed something odd about his results. When he crossed certain species, as a rule, he would get the same hybrid results, but when he crossed *hybrid* plants (having parents with contrasting traits), some of their offspring had odd traits that did not match the parents. This oddity puzzled Mendel, and he decided to try to find an explanation.

Mendel was not the first to notice unusual results when crossing hybrids, of course, but no one ever had reported counting the number of offspring exhibiting the different forms or had tried to classify

Monk and Scientist: Gregor Mendel (1822–1884)

As a boy, Gregor Johann Mendel tended orchard trees for the lord of the manor, and this job early in his life probably started him off on his career as an amateur botanist. He later tutored to earn a living, and finally, in 1843, he entered an Augustinian monastery in Brünn, Moravia, at the age of 21. Since the Augustinians supplied teachers to the schools in Mendel's native Austria, they sent him to the University of Vienna in 1851 to train in mathematics and science. Mendel apparently was a sensitive young man; he failed the examinations three times and had a nervous breakdown, but he finally completed the course and became a teacher in 1854.

Shortly after his university training, Mendel threw himself into what scientists now recognize as one of the greatest experiments in heredity. In the process, from his detailed statistical records, Mendel discerned patterns that no one else had ever reported, and his work should have made a big splash. However, when he read his paper on the results of his experiments to the local natural history society, he met with mild interest.

Disappointed but not defeated, Mendel recognized that he was a completely unknown amateur, and so he thought he might try to gain the sponsorship of a well-known botanist to back him. He sent his paper to the Swiss botanist Karl Wilhelm von Nägeli in 1866. But the paper was too mathematical for Nägeli. To his credit, Nägeli did suspect that evolution came about in jumps, not by "blending" in a smoothly continuous process from generation to generation, but Mendel's

(continues on next page)

Genetics pioneer Gregor Mendel (1822–84) introduced the basic principle of heredity based on his revolutionary scientific experiments conducted in a monastery garden. (The National Library of Medicine)

(continued from previous page)

completely nonspeculative paper did not spark Nägeli's interest.

Yet, Mendel was invited to publish the lectures he had presented in 1865, and they appeared in the Natural History Society's well-received Proceedings in 1866, followed by another publication of his experimental results in 1870. However, only a few people noticed them. For those who did, the articles may have contained either too much botany for those at home in mathematics, or, as with Nägeli, too much math for those more comfortable with botany.

So, some of the most compelling information in the history of genetic science gained comparatively little attention over the next 35 years. Mendel died in 1884 without any idea that one day he would become famous and respected for laying the groundwork for the entire field of genetics.

them. No one had reported trying to keep track of generations, and no one had ever published results as a statistical study. However, to Mendel's mathematical mind, these approaches just seemed logical and in 1865 he presented his key paper on pea hybrids to the Natural History Society in Brünn and was published the following year in the *Proceedings.*

Mendel began to develop a plan. He realized that he would have to raise many generations of many plants to obtain the kind of statistical information he needed. Otherwise, using just a few plants, he would not have a large enough sampling, and he might get misleading results. As he later explained in the introduction to one of his papers, "It indeed required some courage to undertake such far-reaching labors. It appears, however, to be the only way in which we can finally reach the solution of a problem which is of great importance in the evolution of organic forms."

From 1856 to 1864, he grew peas in the monastery garden, carefully keeping records of the traits from generation to generation. There, this unassuming Augustinian monk became the first person to formulate the cardinal principles of heredity. He conducted meticulous experiments in hybridization, carefully examining and recording details about thousands of plants—and his best-known observations were made with garden peas.

He used peas because, over time, gardeners had succeeded in breeding pure strains—for example, they had developed dwarf peas that always bred dwarf plants and tall peas that always bred tall plants. Moreover, peas were self-fertilizing but also could be cross-fertilizing. This allowed for some interesting experimentation. He chose seven pairs of traits to observe that were easily identifiable and sharply contrasted, such as tall plants and dwarf plants, smooth seeds and wrinkled seeds, green *cotyledon*s (the first embryonic plant leaf to appear from a sprouting seed) and yellow cotyledons, inflated pods and constricted pods, yellow pods and green pods, and so on. Mendel crossed a plant having one of these traits with a plant having the contrasting trait. To do this, he first removed the stamens from a flower to prevent self-fertilizing. He then took a small amount of pollen from a plant with the contrasting trait and placed the pollen on the stigma of the flower. Next he wrapped the flower to prevent any further fertilization via wind or insect. The cross-fertilized plant would bear seeds, which he collected, cataloged, and replanted to observe what traits would appear in the next generation. Later he tried cross-fertilizing these hybrids with each other to see what would happen, always keeping careful records and noting what traits the offspring had. He repeated his experiment many times.

In the process, Mendel found that if he crossed pure tall plants with pure dwarf plants, the hybrids that resulted were all tall. They looked just like plants produced from two tall plants. It did not matter whether tall or dwarf plants furnished the male or female germ;

the results appeared to be all the same. The trait that displayed (in this case "tall") Mendel called the *dominant* trait; the trait that did not show in this first hybrid generation (in this case "short") he called *recessive*. Next he crossed two of the hybrid plants together (both of which looked tall but had a dwarf parent). He did several hundred of these crosses and found that he got some dwarf plants and some tall plants as a result. He counted them and worked out the ratio. There were 787 tall plants and 277 short ones—roughly three times as many tall plants as dwarf plants (3:1). His results worked out as shown on the chart on the following page.

Mendel found the identical statistical distribution (give or take a few insignificant percentage points) for all seven traits he studied. He had, of course, focused on simple traits that had only two alternative forms. However, because he had done that, he was readily able to perceive the pattern produced when he traced how parental traits were passed to their offspring. What emerged was the recognition that, while individuals exhibit many differences on the surface, beneath the surface even more complex differences existed. "It can be seen," Mendel later concluded, "how rash it may be to draw from the external resemblances conclusions as to their internal nature." Rash, at least, without careful controls, large numbers of offspring, statistical analysis, and a big dose of caution.

Mendel did not stop with the first generation of hybrids (those whose parents differed with respect to the tested trait); he continued some experiments as far as five or six generations. Later generations produced different but always consistent ratios. He also tried testing more than one trait at once, and as a result of his extensive experiments, he came up with conclusions that have since become known as the two Mendelian principles: the principle of segregation and the principle of independent assortment.

According to the principle of segregation, in sexually reproducing organisms (including plants) two units of heredity control each trait. When the reproductive cells are formed, though, the two units become separated (segregated) from each other, so that the offspring gets one unit for each trait from each parent. Mendel's work gave the first indication that inheritance might be carried by discrete particles in this way (which it is) and not blended.

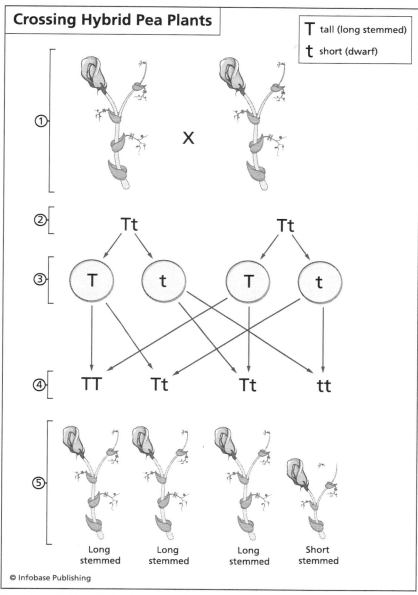

Crossing Hybrid Pea Plants

T tall (long stemmed)
t short (dwarf)

① X

② Tt   Tt

③ T   t   T   t

④ TT   Tt   Tt   tt

⑤ Long stemmed   Long stemmed   Long stemmed   Short stemmed

© Infobase Publishing

*Mendel studied two distinctive forms of one trait, such as a cross between two tall (long-stemmed) hybrid pea plants: (1) each plant looked tall and (2) each plant had both a dominant gene (**T**, tall) and a recessive gene (**t**, dwarf). Further, (3) each gamete had either a dominant gene (**T**) or a recessive gene (**t**), (4) each offspring received one gene from each parent (**T or t**, each circled in (3)). Every tall (5) appearing offspring included at least one gene for tall (**T**) (statistically 3 out of 4).*

When reproductive cells are formed, according to the principle of independent assortment, the distribution of the units of heredity for each trait does not interfere with the distribution of others. For example, he found that he could produce either tall or short pea plants that bore wrinkled peas and either short or tall pea plants with smooth peas.

Admittedly, Mendel may have come up with this clear, uncluttered picture as a matter of luck. However, the particular traits he chose in the pea plant had distinct, discontinuous variations for each pair, with no intermediate grades. Each was simple, not controlled by more than one hereditary unit. As a result he did not end up, for example, with any offspring pea plants that were of medium height instead of tall or short. In humans, we now know that both height and skin color are controlled by several genes. So it is possible to get intermediate height and shades of skin color. Albinism (the absence of skin pigment) is a simple two-gene trait in humans, however, like Mendel's models. So a father and mother having normal skin color but each carrying a gene for the recessive trait of albinism could have a child that had no skin pigmentation at all. (In fact, the chances would be one in four.)

In addition, Mendel happened to choose traits that appeared not to be linked in any way—although two of the genes he studied were far apart, so they appeared to be unlinked when they actually were. So none of the odd results caused by what is now known as *linkage* occurred in his studies. (More on that subject later.) So, while his principle of independent assortment still applies, it holds only for those traits that are not linked.

Mendel Rediscovered

Between the time Mendel did his work and the beginning of the 20th century, two important advances—improved microscopes and improved cell staining—opened up the nucleus of the cell to inspection and made possible an examination of hereditary factors at a different level. As a result, scientists began examining the cell nucleus and discovered that clusters of rods appeared shortly before cell division. These rods, or *chromosomes,* as they became named, seemed to split in two lengthwise—although they actually duplicated—and the two sets that resulted went separate ways into the two halves of the dividing cell. Then the chromosomes rolled up into a ball and seemed to disappear. However, no one knew what role chromosomes played.

In 1900, a Dutch botanist named Hugo de Vries recognized that British evolutionary scientist Charles Darwin (1809–82) had not explained in his theory of evolution how individuals might vary and pass these variances on. So de Vries began work on a *hypothesis* about how different characteristics might vary independently of each other and recombine in many different combinations. He concluded from his study of the evening primrose (*Oenothera lamarckiana*) that new traits, or mutations, can appear suddenly and can be inherited, having found certain types of this plant that seemed substantially different from the original wild plant. Through experimentation, he found that these substantially different forms also bred true thereafter. Before publishing his findings, de Vries looked back through the literature already published on his subject, and to his amazement, he stumbled across the papers Mendel had published in the 1860s.

Coincidentally, two other scientists, one in Austria and one in Germany, also came across Mendel's work almost simultaneously. To the credit of all three, not one of them tried to claim Mendel's work as his own. All three published Mendel's results, giving him full credit, and each added his own name only as a confirmation.

Some of the variations observed by de Vries were not actually mutations, as he thought, but hybrid combinations. Still, the evidence for the theory from other sources reinforced his concept of mutations. Actually, mutations had long been commonly observed and used in breeding by those who raised cattle, sheep, and other domestic stock. Unfortunately, little exchange went on between the scientific community and herders. So when Hugo de Vries published a book, *Mutationslehre,* in 1901, advancing the belief that evolution is due to sudden jumps or mutations (from a Latin word meaning "to change"), it was news. He commonly receives credit for the initiation of this line of investigation into the causes of evolution.

Fruit Fly Geneticist: Thomas Hunt Morgan (1866–1945)

Descended from an illustrious southern family (nephew of a Confederate general and related to Francis Scott Key, the author of the U.S. national anthem), Thomas Hunt Morgan was born September 25, 1866, in Lexington, Kentucky. Two decades later, in 1886, he earned his B.S. degree from the State College of Kentucky (which later became the University of Kentucky) and, after receiving his Ph.D. from the Johns Hopkins University in 1890, he joined the faculty of Bryn Mawr College. By 1904, he was professor of experimental zoology at Columbia University, where he set up a large lab that soon became known as the "Fly Room."

There, with the help of a team of graduate assistants and his wife, biologist Lilian Morgan (née Vaughan Sampson), Thomas Hunt Morgan and his colleagues took advantage of two characteristics of the fruit fly, also known as the vinegar fly (Latin name: *Drosophila melanogaster*). First, a fruit fly can propagate a large generation of offspring in two weeks. So this meant that, instead of waiting for the next growing season the way Mendel had to do with his peas, the experimental scientists working in the Fly Room could see as many as 30 generations and their inherited traits in a year. Second, the fruit fly has only four chromosomes. This meant that only a few different combinations were possible, and so it was easier to show how a gene located on one of those chromosomes could pass on a trait from one generation to another. In this way, Morgan and his students were easily able to see the results of mating individual flies having specific characteristics. This early work was among the first to carry Mendel's genetics from the plant world into the animal world.

For his contributions to classical genetics, Morgan would win the Nobel prize in physiology or medicine in 1933.

Thomas Hunt Morgan, the Drosophila team leader who headed the "Fly Room" at Columbia University, received the Nobel prize in 1933 for his contributions to the study of chromosomes and their role in heredity. (The National Library of Medicine)

Bateson and Gene Linkage

When English biologist William Bateson (1861–1926) read the papers by Mendel that de Vries had found, he was impressed. He became a staunch supporter of the Mendelian legacy and translated the papers into English. In 1905, he also took Mendel's work a step further based on his own experiments with inherited characteristics. He found that not all characteristics were inherited independently—some were linked, or inherited together—and he published his results in 1905.

By then the study of the mechanism of inheritance was gaining stature and a substantial literature, and Bateson proposed the name *genetics* for the growing new field. He was the first person anywhere to be appointed to the position of professor of genetics, a title he accepted at Cambridge University in 1908. However, American scientist Thomas Hunt Morgan was the one who would explain how gene linkage worked.

Fruit-Fly Genetics

Few studies in genetics have been as productive as Thomas Hunt Morgan's work with the fruit fly (*Drosophila*), and one of his greatest inspirations was to use this small, easily bred creature to test his ideas about inherited characteristics and how they are passed on from generation to generation.

Mendel's work had just been rediscovered a couple of years earlier. Those who had observed the behavior of chromosomes in dividing cells and egg formation were talking about how close the fit was between this process and the results Mendel had published. However, there was a disparity between the complexity of inherited traits and the number of chromosomes. For example, while the human organism is highly complex, the human cell has only 23 pairs of chromosomes. Morgan saw that Bateson was right: These few structures could not account for the thousands of characteristics in the human body, unless there was some smaller structure, carrying some large number of factors, at work within the chromosome.

Ironically, as late as 1908, Morgan agreed with skeptics of Mendel's work, one of whom remarked, "There is no definite proof of *Mendelism* [the science of inheritance as put forth by Mendel] applying to any living form at present." However, Morgan became curious about the process of mutation, and he looked around for a good species to study, just as Mendel had found the garden pea. He settled finally on the *Drosophila,* a small fruit fly that breeds with great rapidity, has clearly marked mutations, has only four pairs of chromosomes, and is easy to feed on a mash of bananas. Morgan found he could breed 30 generations in a year. Soon Morgan's laboratory at Columbia University overflowed with jars of flies.

Despite close daily examination, Morgan could not find any mutations in his flies. He subjected the flies to both high and low temperatures. He exposed them to acids, alkalis, and radioactivity. He fed them unusual diets. Still no mutants. Then one day in April 1910, after a year of watching and waiting, Lilian Morgan (or possibly another researcher), spotted a fly with abnormal white eyes: *Drosophila* normally has red eyes. Morgan had been waiting for this mutant. He bred his white-eyed male with normal red-eyed females. Soon he had 1,237 offspring, but every one had red eyes. However, among following generations, out of 4,252 flies, 798 had white eyes. He had succeeded in perpetuating mutation!

These statistics were puzzling, however. First, the ratio was not the ratio of 3:1 that Mendel had found in his hybrid peas. What is more, all of the white-eyed flies were male. When Morgan and his team examined this question further, they realized that the trait of white eyes was sex-linked: They had found the first linked traits in *Drosophila* a complication that Mendel's clearly segregated traits had not raised. Genetic linkage (when two or more traits consistently appear together) was codiscovered by British geneticist William Bateson and Reginald Punnett. However, this was a sex-linked mutation, and Morgan and his team used this discovery as a tool for finding out more about how genes work. During the two years following Morgan's first paper on sex-linked traits in 1910, he published 13 more about 20 or so sex-linked mutations in *Drosophila.* The sex-linked mutations made possible an unusually focused study of "transmission genetics."

By this time, researchers had recognized that genetic material resided on chromosomes and that genes were carried in linear fashion, strung like beads on a string or like links in a chain.

By the end of 1910, Morgan had 40 different kinds of mutants, which he gave names like Humpy, Chubby, Pink-eye, Crumpled, Dumpy, and Speck. Some had no wings, some had no eyes, some had no hair, some had crumpled wings, and so on. For the most part, the mutations were not advantageous, but he found other links. White eyes developed only with yellow wings, never with gray wings. A characteristic he called ebony body went only with pink eyes, and black body went only with yellow wings. Morgan began to realize that certain characteristics were grouped together on the same chromosome.

Then one day, strangely, white eyes showed up in flies that did not have yellow wings. This was a real puzzler. Morgan boldly hypothesized that maybe the broken piece of chromosome had crossed over to reassemble with another chromosome. If this were so, a whole group of traits could be expected to be linked to another group of traits with which they had never before typically been linked. As it turned out, that is exactly what proved to be the case. This event became known as "crossing-over," and it would play an important part in some of Barbara McClintock's work just a few years later.

Morgan's work style typified the teamwork that became more and more prevalent in

This photo of a pair of vinegar flies (Drosophila, sometimes called a fruit fly) compares a spectacular mutant array of four wings (top) to the normal, two-winged vinegar fly (bottom). (California Institute of Technology)

20th-century science, incorporating the specialized talents of several scientists, including Alfred Sturtevant, a specialist in mathematical analysis of the results achieved through breeding the *Drosophila* and mapping of genetic factors on chromosomes; Hermann Muller, a theorist who also had a talent for designing experiments; and Calvin Bridges, who was especially adept at studying cells. They worked both independently and as a unit, sharing results and collaborating on experiments. Together they worked out the idea that Mendel's factors, as he had called them, were specific physical units, or genes, with definite locations on the chromosome.

With Sturtevant, Muller, and Bridges, Morgan published *The Mechanism of Mendelian Heredity* in 1915, providing an analysis and synthesis of Mendelian inheritance as formulated from the author team's epoch-making investigations. A classic work, the book has become a cornerstone of modern interpretation of heredity.

Morgan would soon establish gene theory in his book *The Theory of the Gene,* published in 1926. In this work, he would complete Mendel's work as far as it could be taken with the tools available—brain, eye, and microscope. A year later, Muller would use ionizing radiation (X-rays) to probe *Drosophila*'s genetic mysteries, publishing in 1927, while Lewis Stadler, who did post-doctoral work at Cornell and would later be important to McClintock's career, published his work with radiation and maize a year after that, in 1928. These cutting-edge events would occur within the decade as McClintock began her undergraduate studies in fall 1919. The advent of molecular biology and the work of Francis Crick and James Watson on DNA were still more than a quarter-century away.

When Cells Divide

Cell division is key to understanding McClintock's work, specifically the two different ways that cells divide: *mitosis* and *meiosis.* Cells are the building blocks that make up living things, and within each cell is a central headquarters, the nucleus, where the central players of genetics reside. Mendel knew there were controlling units, or elements, as he called them, but he did not know where or what they were. In 1909, Danish botanist Wilhelm Johanssen gave them the name *genes* (from a Greek word meaning "to give birth to"), a spin-off from the name *genetics* that Bateson gave the related field of science.

Mitosis is the common process that divides a cell into two duplicate, or daughter, cells having the same number of chromosomes as the original, parent cell. Meiosis is a special form of cell division that takes place in organisms that reproduce sexually (including plants). During meiosis, two successive cell divisions take place, ultimately producing four daughter cells and reducing the number of chromosomes in each nucleus to half the number in the parent cell's nucleus. The original number of chromosomes is known as the *diploid* number (2n), and the resulting reduced number is known as the *haploid* number (n).

Flowering plants (such as the garden peas grown by Mendel and McClintock's maize) undergo meiosis in the *sporophyte* phase (a spore-producing diploid [2n] stage) to produce haploid spores. This process is called *sporogenesis*. Haploid spores (n, the products of meiosis) divide by mitosis and develop into a *gamete*-producing stage or phase called a *gametophyte* (n). Haploid gametophytes undergo mitosis to produce gametes (sex cells, n). This process is called *gametogenesis*. Haploid *gametes* (male or female sex cells) may fuse with a gamete from another gametophyte to form diploid *zygotes* (2n). Each zygote will divide by mitosis to form an embryo, which will later develop (by mitosis) into a sporophyte phase and begin the life cycle again. This type of life cycle is known as the alternation of generations, because the plant has both haploid and diploid forms during its lifetime.

Mitosis and meiosis are sometimes described as "the dance of the chromosomes," as these stringy forms seem to follow a silent musical score and elaborate choreography. (When researchers stained cells for observation under a microscope, these small bodies absorbed the color of the stain, and so they were named *chromosomes* ["colored bodies"].)

In mitosis, as the diploid cell prepares to divide, the chromosomes pair up in sets—aligned at the center, one from each parent. A football-shaped structure known as a spindle forms: Poles form

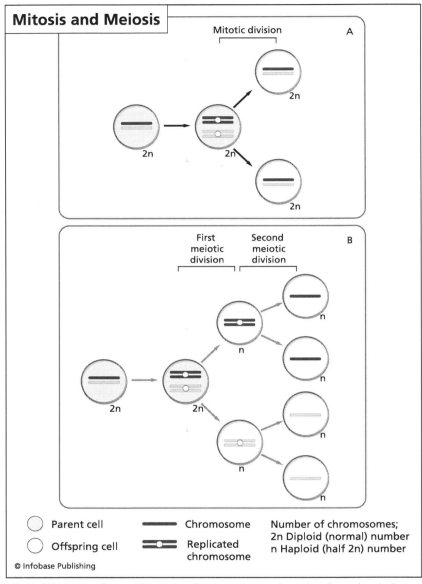

Mitosis and Meiosis

Mitotic division — A

First meiotic division — Second meiotic division — B

Parent cell
Offspring cell
Chromosome
Replicated chromosome
Number of chromosomes;
2n Diploid (normal) number
n Haploid (half 2n) number

© Infobase Publishing

Mitosis (A) is generally used by an organism to replace and repair cells, and meiosis (B) is generally associated with reproduction. Mitosis produces offspring cells, called diploid, having two sets of chromosomes (2n), and resembling the parent cell. Meiosis produces offspring cells, called haploid, with half the normal number (n) of chromosomes. In animals, meiosis produces haploid cells, called gametes (ovum or sperm). In flowering plants, such as peas and maize, meiosis produces haploid cells, called spores. Each haploid spore nucleus divides by mitosis to produce gametes (egg or sperm).

at opposing ends of the cell, connected by tiny fibers that arc from pole to pole like lines of longitude on a globe. Lined up along the equator, the paired chromosomes separate and slip in opposite directions along the spindle fibers to opposite poles. Then the cell divides along the equator, forming two daughter cells with identical sets of paired chromosomes. This chromosomal or genetic condition is known as a *diploid* cell or diploid plant. Each species has a typical diploid number. For example, maize cells contain 10 paired chromosomes, for a diploid number of 20 and the plant is referred to as a diploid plant.

In many ways meiosis is a similar process, but meiosis results in four daughter cells each containing only half the chromosomes contained in the parent cell. In animals, meiosis produces haploid cells (gametes, sex cells) directly. In flowering plants, however, meiosis produces haploid cells (spores, n), which then undergo mitosis to produce gametes. The final products emerging from this process contain only one set of chromosomes—one-half of each pair (a *haploid*)—for a total of 10 chromosomes for maize. Later on, when fertilization occurs, haploid gametes (derived from each parent) fuse to form a normal diploid cell (zygote).

Belgian cytologist F. A. Janssens observed in 1909 that sometimes during prophase (the first stage) in meiosis, a pair of chromosomes would appear to be stuck together in one place along their length, forming an X, which he called *chiasma* (plural: *chiasmata*). Pairs of chromosomes that formed chiasmata appeared to exchange segments in a process that became known as crossing over—a process that would become significant to McClintock's work in the coming decades.

Exploring the Genetics of Maize

While many geneticists had their eyes on Thomas Hunt Morgan and his Fly Room in the 1920s, a considerable number of researchers around the country saw advantages in studying maize (Indian corn). True, the vinegar fly had a short life span and researchers could track many generations in a year, but flies' chromosomes were not that easy to study. They were small, and inherited traits were difficult to see without a microscope. Also, up until the discovery in 1933 of *Drosophila*'s large salivary gland chromosome, even a microscope offered little help to cytologists.

At first glance, though, maize was an even less desirable object of study. Maize had a longer life cycle, producing only one generation in an entire year. (Crops raised in a greenhouse—or in a tropical climate—might produce two generations a year, but that was still painfully slow.) So results and statistics took longer to obtain. Researchers could not see many identifying characteristics that could help them distinguish one chromosome from another, and they were not even sure how many there were because different strains had different numbers of chromosomes. Finally, the genetics of maize plants was far more complex and difficult than the genetics of *Drosophila*.

So why did so many researchers like studying maize? First, maize fell naturally in the territory of botanists who had defined the cutting edge of genetics and cytogenetics. Gregor Mendel, after all, was a botanist, and so were Hugo de Vries and Wilhelm Johanssen. These scientists had formed the foundation of genetic research. However, there were several more practical attractions. Maize was a centuries-old food crop that growers and botanists had been observing carefully throughout this extensive history. Most of all, maize chromosomes had many distinct characteristics, as it would turn out, and extra chromosomes occur frequently—making maize plants perfect for the study of cytogenetics.

In addition, researchers began to find that they could make the complexity of maize biology work for, instead of against, them. The complexity has made maize research harder for nonbotanists to follow. Yet this complexity has also provided some advantages to researchers. Unlike animals, each plant produces both male and female *gametes* (germ cells). The *sperm* cell (male gamete) is located in pollen grains in the tassel at the top of the stalk. The *ovum* (egg cell, the female gamete) is located in the ovule at the base of the silks (soft, silky strands emerging from the stalk at the place where an ear of corn kernels will grow). In nature, pollen grains (containing nuclei) sperm sometimes fall from the tassel, land on the silks, and self-pollinate and self-fertilize the plant, or

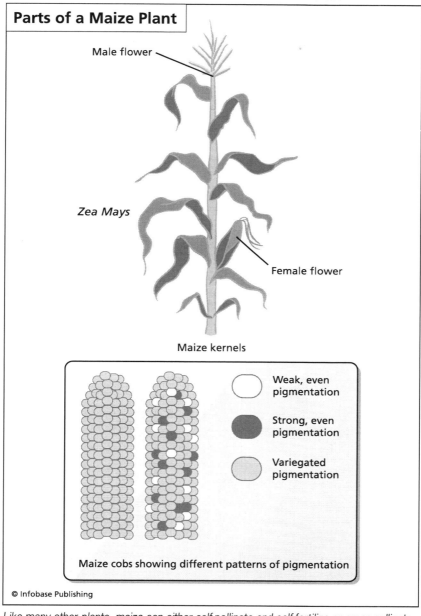

Parts of a Maize Plant

Male flower

Zea Mays

Female flower

Maize kernels

Weak, even pigmentation

Strong, even pigmentation

Variegated pigmentation

Maize cobs showing different patterns of pigmentation

© Infobase Publishing

Like many other plants, maize can either self-pollinate and self-fertilize or cross-pollinate and cross-fertilize. In nature, the pollen (containing the gametes) falls on the female flowers, and the embryo begins development in the kernels, or seeds, that form on the cobs. The patterns of pigmentation in these kernels were of great interest to McClintock for studying how genetic differences affect traits in the offspring.

they may travel on winds, water, animals, birds, or insects, fertilizing neighboring plants. Once fertilized, an embryo begins to form, protected by an ovary wall fused with a seed coat and furnished with food (the endosperm). This becomes the corn kernel (the edible part).

For McClintock and other maize researchers, the presence of both male and female gametes allowed study of the parents' genetics. They could also examine both the embryo and the parent maize plant for a contrast of parent and daughter genetics. And the endosperm (food for the embryo) was composed of tissue formed by a second sperm fertilizing two twins of the egg. This arrangement allowed special insights into the dominance and recessive aspects of a gene's influence on inheritance.

However, as McClintock began her graduate studies, much progress was hindered by the need for improved techniques. Without them, maize researchers could not explore the intricate dance of the chromosomes (where the answers to many genetic questions lay)—at least not yet.

Getting Started: Freedom to Work (1923–1927)

For Barbara McClintock, genetics was an especially exciting field to enter in the 1920s. It was complex, challenging, and cutting-edge. Many questions clamored for answers from enterprising young scientists, and Cornell's College of Agriculture, where McClintock was enrolled, was a particularly fertile environment. Members of the faculty were accessible and supportive both in class and out.

One botany professor, Lester W. Sharp, even met with McClintock, as she recalled, on Saturdays for a private seminar on techniques in cytology. Combined with her own natural skills, this kind of individual training made a key contribution to her development as a scientist. Because of the level of skill she attained, she soon became Sharp's assistant in his cytology class.

McClintock received her bachelor of science degree in 1923 and was eager to begin her graduate work. To her, continuing with her work at Cornell was only logical. The question "What next?" never came up. Sharp became her thesis adviser and, trusting her instincts as a researcher, he gave her free rein in the laboratory. "He just left me free to do anything I wanted to do, just completely free," she later remarked in an interview with biographer Evelyn Fox Keller. Working with chromosomes under a microscope was her strongest talent, and she loved it. She also knew that a great deal of work remained to be done on chromosomes, so her choice was obvious, and she plunged right in.

A natural at the microscope, McClintock awed her fellow students (and her colleagues later in her career), and she frequently found herself teaching them her techniques. In an interview with Keller, Marcus Rhoades recalled once exclaiming to McClintock "I've often marveled that you can look at a cell under the microscope and can see so much!" "Well, you know," he said she replied in her forthright style, "when I look at a cell, I get down in that cell and look around." She later expanded on that comment: "You're not conscious of anything else. . . . You are so absorbed that even small things get big. . . . Nothing else matters. You're noticing more and more things that most people couldn't see because they didn't go intensely over each part, slowly but with great intensity. . . . It's the intensity of your absorption. . . ."

Ten Maize Chromosomes

In 1924, early in McClintock's career, when she was a graduate student, she took a job as a paid assistant to Lowell F. Randolph, a Cornell doctorate who had obtained a United States Department of Agriculture (USDA) position at Cornell in 1923. The pairing looked promising to Rollins Emerson, who always encouraged openness and data sharing, not only among his students and colleagues at Cornell, but among all researchers in his field.

Emerson saw that a great deal of progress could be made by pairing researchers who had plant breeding backgrounds with those who possessed the laboratory and analysis capabilities inherent in a cytological background, especially in the new and growing field of cytogenetics. Randolph had both, having studied plant breeding as a minor under Emerson with his major in cytology under Sharp, completing his Ph.D. at Cornell in 1921. Emerson probably had hopes that McClintock and Randolph would work well together—on, for example, a systematic study of maize linkages or similar projects that would contribute to the strength of Cornell's contribution in the field. But it would not be possible to do maize cytogenetics until each maize chromosome could be identified, a project in which Randolph had great interest (as Lee Kass and Christophe Bonneuil discuss in their 2004 article).

In February 1925, McClintock settled on her Ph.D. thesis topic: the "B," or accessory, chromosomes of corn, a topic that had intrigued Randolph. However, like many a thesis topic, this one did not last long. That summer, McClintock found an even more interesting topic: a "triploid" maize plant found in the Cornell cornfields. A triploid plant is an uncommon specimen having three complete sets of chromosomes in every cell. It could form, for example, if a diploid sperm (having two complete sets of chromosomes) fused with a haploid ovum (having one complete set of chromosomes), producing an embryo having three sets of chromosomes.

McClintock's training and studies as assistant in Sharp's cytology class had offered her a thorough exposure to the history and techniques of staining—a method for accentuating cellular structures for microscopic studies. Randolph and Sharp had learned a new staining technique developed by cytologist John Belling—descriptively known as the "squash" technique. Belling's find called for fixing cells on a slide, staining them with a carmine stain, and then applying the glass cover with the thumb to flatten them carefully so the inner structure could be seen. Together, Randolph and McClintock used the smear technique to analyze the chromosomes of the pollen parent cells from the triploid plant. They also developed a hypothesis for how this unusual plant came to be, and they published their results in the *American Naturalist* in February 1926.

Their teamwork ended there, as Lee Kass discovered, because McClintock felt she had done most of the work and should have received first listing as coauthor. As a result, a distancing developed between her and the Plant Breeding Department, where Randolph's side of the story probably received a friendlier hearing, if only because he was working closely with Emerson.

The two had also disagreed about a practice McClintock apparently had of jumping in to solve a problem without an invitation In addition, Randolph's progress on the problem of identifying the maize chromosomes was blocked because he could only determine large from small maize chromosomes and had not yet found a method for seeing distinguishing characteristics between chromosomes of different sizes. There was also controversy about the base number of chromosomes for maize because different strains had different base numbers and researchers had reported different numbers for various strains of maize.

McClintock, who always loved a good puzzle, decided to try her hand. Later she would remark, "Well, I discovered a way in which he could do it, and I had it done within two or three days—the whole thing done, clear, sharp, and nice." But as science historian Lee B. Kass pointed out in correspondence with the authors, the project "took a long time—[it was] not so easy." In fact, Kass points out, while tradition has it that McClintock solved the problem while still a graduate student, she did not succeed in solving several important aspects until 1928–29, after she had completed her Ph.D. in 1927 and after Randolph published a paper in 1928 establishing the base number of chromosomes as 10. Meanwhile, upon receiving her doctorate, to put food on the table, she accepted an appointment as an instructor at Cornell.

By 1929, her thesis was published in *Genetics,* a key journal in the field. She also found time, between teaching assignments, to succeed in finding two new angles on the stubborn problem of chromosome morphology. First, as she said, she looked in a different place. Randolph had been studying maize chromosomes during what appeared to be the best opportunity—the metaphase, when they appeared to get larger and fatter and, therefore, easier to see. McClintock also made successful use of the metaphase stage to find identifying characteristics on the chromosomes. As an instructor, McClintock figured out a way to use the metaphase of mitotic haploid chromosomes in the first division of the developing pollen grain—the gametophyte (n) stage—to identify the 10 maize chromosomes. She especially noticed that she could tell how each chromosome differed in length in these mitotic haploid chromosomes: She saw that a narrowing, the centromere, occurred in different locations on different chromosomes, creating arms of different lengths. One even had a sort of satellite, or moon, attached to the main strand by a slender thread, or stalk. In fact, it so happened that all 10 chromosomes had clearly recognizable *morphological* (structural) markers, serving to orient the traveler like a street sign or, more aptly put, like a landmark. She published these findings as a short but major article in the prestigious journal *Science,* announcing the haploid number (10) of chromosomes found in maize as well as a diagram, known as an ideogram, of all 10 chromosomes.

This one feat alone showed McClintock's early accomplishment, but she had in mind doing much more. Her success with identifying the maize mitotic haploid chromosomes, published in 1929, was just beginning, and in the next three years, she continued to produce a series of papers that, in the words of geneticist Marcus Rhoades, "clearly established her as the foremost investigator in cytogenetics." Thanks to McClintock's knowledge, experience, and unusual talents, with a little practice she soon became expert at Belling's stain technique. By making a few wizardly adjustments to improve the clarity of results for maize, she succeeded in gathering a highly viewable sample of every chromosome at each stage of cell division and replication in both mitotic and meiotic chromosomes.

By 1929–30, she also had the idea of looking at the process of cell division during the pachytene stage of meiosis. During this stage, in certain strains of corn, the chromosomes are more slender and stretched out and less condensed. McClintock found that the chromosomes were much easier to study before they became so dense. She also could see a narrowing at the area where the two chromatids attached themselves to the stretched-out spindle fibers. While observing chromosomes in the pachytene stage, in corn plants provided by Dr. C. R. Burnham, she also observed a knobby structure on some chromosomes. The absence or presence and location of these knobs offered another way to tell the chromosomes apart. (For more information, see Kass and Bonneuil's paper published in 2004 and Kass's 2003 publication on this subject.)

McClintock was therefore able to identify the different maize chromosomes in 1929, and by 1933, in pachytene stages, the chromosomes were numbered 1 through 10, from longest to shortest, by contrasting their shapes, measuring their lengths, and comparing their patterns. This important episode in her early career already showed her uncanny ability to combine flawless laboratory technique with visual acuity, sure-footed interpretation of what she saw, and highly cerebral and imaginative integration of all the pieces to a complex puzzle.

Scientist at Work

(1927–1931)

Barbara McClintock began her research career knowing exactly what she wanted to do: explore cytogenetics or, in other words, work with chromosomes and their genetic content and expressions. For fruit flies, researchers had already discovered that specific linked genes were always carried on the same chromosome. —as in the case of Morgan's White Eye, which was also always male, showing a link between the white eye and the male gender. McClintock wanted to do the same work on maize, associating particular linkage groups with particular chromosomes, or, put more broadly, integrating the study of chromosomes with the study of genes.

Often, the plants she would study were grown for her by colleagues such as George Beadle and Marcus Rhoades, who planted and grew the maize plants, tending them as necessary for producing the crosses she needed. In addition to her skills with a microscope, though, she would also develop a thorough knowledge of the plant in all its stages by spending time working in the fields. From this exposure she developed a deep, thorough knowledge of the maize plant. Like Sherlock Holmes, she would develop the ability to glance at a plant and read its story instantly, based on the minute details she observed both from the macroscopic view, the external features of the plant's morphology, and from the microscopic view, which enabled her to detect tomes of information about the plant's chromosomes and genes and the roles they play in producing the external features.

The Cornell Cytogenetics Group

Despite her independence, McClintock soon found herself at the center of a group of colleagues who joined forces in a cooperative effort—bouncing ideas off each other and sharing insights and techniques. It all started spontaneously with the arrivals of George Beadle (in the summer of 1926) and Marcus Rhoades (in September 1928). Both were doctoral students who studied with top maize geneticist Rollins A. Emerson.

Rhoades had received his bachelor's degree in botany and mathematics from the University of Michigan. Plant geneticist E. G. Anderson had taken him under his wing and had introduced him to Emerson, under whom Anderson had studied at Cornell. Rhoades spent three of his graduate years living as a "member of the family" in Rollins's home in Ithaca. Rhoades also spent one year of his graduate training at the California Institute of Technology (Caltech), where he worked further with Anderson, who, like Morgan, moved there. Morgan brought with him his cutting-edge *Drosophila* studies as well as his team, including Morgan himself, as well as Alfred Sturtevant (mathematical analysis), Theodosius Dobzhansky (Ukrainian zoologist-geneticist), and C. B. Bridges (geneticist). So, in the process, Rhoades probably became well informed about the work in genetics that was already under way on *Drosophila*.

On arrival, Rhoades was curious about what kind of work was going on in his new environment, so he went into the big laboratory room where several people were working and found McClintock working at a small table. He asked what she was working on, and when she told him about her project, he was immediately interested and, as McClintock later told the story, "... he became very excited and went around and explained to the others the significance of what I was trying to do. As a consequence, I was taken back into the fold."

Rhoades and McClintock were immediately in tune with each other intellectually. No one else seemed to understand the path she was taking and why she wanted to travel that path. Rhoades understood instantly. He also saw that he had found his own path in the field of maize cytogenetics. McClintock's experience and insights would provide the entry he needed. Most of the graduate students in botany in the late 1920s had come to study with Emerson. He was a distinguished scientist, recognized as the top geneticist then studying corn genetics through breeding. He challenged his students to work hard, and he rewarded them with a remarkable freedom and enthusiastic interest. But to Rhoades, McClintock's work was the most exciting project at Cornell. She was traveling on the cutting edge, on a new frontier. From that first day forward, McClintock and Rhoades formed a strong, mutually beneficial bond that would last a lifetime. (Rhoades later became nationally respected for his work in maize genetics. Elected to vice president and then president of the Genetics Society of America, he served for years as editor of the journal *Genetics*.)

McClintock also hit it off with George Beadle, who would later share the Nobel Prize in physiology or medicine with Edward Tatum and Joshua Lederberg in 1958 for his work in the field of molecular genetics verifying the "one gene/one enzyme" hypothesis. Born in Wahoo, Nebraska, Beadle had grown up in the cornfields of Nebraska and attended the University of Nebraska. He would become another strong ally for McClintock.

McClintock, Rhoades, and Beadle formed the core of a group of researchers who began to focus on proving the basic postulates of plant genetics—such as the physical presence of genes on chromosomes. For *Drosophila*, much of this had already been done. Now they would undertake the job for *Zea mays* (maize). A few other researchers joined the group later, but McClintock, Rhoades,

These corn geneticists in the Plant Breeding Department, Cornell University, 1929, were colleagues of Barbara McClintock and many were members of the core group she headed. Top row, left to right: Rollins Adams Emerson, unidentified, Marcus M. Rhoades, Harold M. Perry, L. F. Randolph, Charles Russell Burnham. Bottom row, left to right: Hsien W. Li, George Beadle, Ernest Dorsey. (Researched by Lee B. Kass; the Maize Genetics Cooperation Newsletter 78 (2004). Available online. URL: http://www.agron.missouri.edu/mnl/78/04kass.html. The Barbara McClintock Papers, American Philosophical Society)

and Beadle always formed the core. They held their own seminars, ate lunch together in the cornfields, and explored the topics and issues related to their interests (often without a professor present), discussing nonstop the relationship between chromosomes and genes and generally all facets of cytogenetics, including those being revealed or suggested by their own efforts. Describing the group as "close-knit" and "self-sustaining," McClintock wrote in her brief Nobel autobiography, "Credit for its success rests with Professor Emerson who quietly ignored some of our seemingly strange behaviors." For all, it was a profoundly stimulating experience, and the period that followed is considered the Cornell maize group's "golden age," under Barbara McClintock's able leadership.

Rhoades and Beadle represented two contrasting takes on McClintock from those days that were probably also common in others who worked with her. Rhoades had a consistent respect for McClintock's intellect. "One thing that's to my credit," he would later recall, "—that I recognized from the start that she was good, that she was much better than I was . . ." Beadle also made a similar remark years later: "My enthusiasm was shared—so much so in the case of Barbara

A key member of the Cornell genetics group, Marcus Rhoades remained a lifelong friend to McClintock and a supportive colleague. (Indiana University)

McClintock that it was difficult to dissuade her from interpreting all my cytological preparations. Of course, she could do this much more effectively than I."

Everyone agreed that McClintock was smart. Rhoades considered her clearly "something special," and Beadle used expressions such as "fantastic," "spectacular," and "the best job that's been done." "I've known a lot of famous scientists," Rhoades remarked in a 1980 interview. "But the only one I thought really was a genius was McClintock."

Her brilliance was a given, but some people found her irritating and difficult. She continued to beat people at their own work, as she did with Fitz Randolph and George Beadle, and some people took offense, feeling that she was unfair or unwanted competition and stole their work and their opportunity to gain recognition. In Beadle's case, he and McClintock ended up publishing the results jointly in 1928 in a note in *Science*. He did complain to Emerson, though, who was department chair. According to McClintock, Emerson "told him that he should be grateful there was someone around who could explain it. The fun was solving problems, like a game," she added according to science writer Sharon Bertsch McGrayne. "It was entertaining."

Beyond the personal level, McClintock and her cadre of cytogeneticists differed in approach and orientation from the old-school geneticists who approached the study of inheritance in botany through the study of inherited traits by controlled breeding. The older group had not had a chance to get used to the approach that McClintock and her colleagues were taking. Further, they were not used to the level of accuracy and detail McClintock used to obtain her results. This caused a continuing rift between her and the "old school." Even she apparently thought of the situation as a battle of the generations, declaring that older people could not join the group because they did not have the same intensity about their work.

Intensity the cytology group definitely had, and McClintock especially so. She attacked problems in bursts, working on and off, day and night, until she reached a solution, and she seemed to have boundless energy, taking on physical challenges with the same unflinching will. Sometimes, the stories told about Barbara McClintock are written larger than life, and often facts are not solid. Stories told in interviews—oral history—often are told long after they have occurred and memories have become faded and compressed. Women and girls looking for role models and heroes have embellished true stories. McClintock's own love of a good story has doubtless sometimes augmented a tale. McClintock, a basically private person, occasionally seems to have created facades to hide behind. One such tale writ large is the story of the parched cornfield, as reported by biographer Nathaniel C. Comfort. No proof has turned up to authenticate the tale. No document has ever justified its place in the factual history of this remarkable woman's life. Perhaps something like it did happen. . . . As the tale begins one wants to say, "Once upon a time . . ." When she was in danger of losing an entire crop to a prolonged dry spell, she laid an irrigation line of water pipe up to the hilltop where her cornfield was withering in the hot sun, ignoring her own pain from the blistering work as tears rolled down her cheeks. When a nighttime flood washed out her newly planted kernels, she replanted the entire patch working virtually in the dark except for the dim light offered by a pair of car headlights.

McClintock and Creighton Team Up

In the summer of 1929, a young graduate student in botany arrived on the Cornell campus. Her name was Harriet Creighton. She was 21 years old and a graduate of Wellesley College, a student of Dr. Margaret Ferguson, who had taught science at Wellesley for 26 years. No doubt recognizing intelligence and a talent for science in Creighton, Ferguson had encouraged her to attend graduate school at Cornell.

When Creighton arrived, she was assigned as a graduate teaching assistant to paleobotanist Loren C. Petry in the botany department in the College of Agriculture at Cornell. She was planning to study either plant physiology or cytology. On Creighton's first day, however, she met Barbara McClintock, who immediately began to change Creighton's plans. She set up Sharp as Creighton's adviser and arranged the younger woman's course of study, settling on a major in genetics and cytology and a minor in plant physiology. McClintock advised going straight for a doctorate, skipping the master's degree— an unusual plan at the time, one intended to send a message of commitment and confidence. McClintock took charge—perhaps because Creighton was a woman and McClintock knew there would be obstacles to overcome, perhaps because she saw something of herself in this young student, or perhaps because McClintock was looking ahead to the day when she would leave and Sharp would need a new assistant for his cytogenetics class. Looking back, Creighton thought the last possibility was the most likely. In any case, McClintock handed Creighton a lot of advice, and Creighton listened well. It was the beginning of a lifelong friendship.

Like Charles Burnham, who arrived at Cornell at about the same time, Harriet Creighton was also welcomed into the cytology group formed by McClintock, Rhoades, and Beadle. Creighton soon became an able research partner to McClintock, and McClintock, just two years after completing her own Ph.D., magnanimously operated by a dictum she learned from Rollins Emerson. When handing out a research project to a fresh, new student, he advised, offer "the very best and most promising problem you have." And that is exactly what McClintock did.

The problem offered to Creighton was the challenge to show definitive, physical proof that during meiosis in maize, some of one parent's genes, along with the segment of chromosome on which they were located, physically crossed over to the other parent's *homologous* (similar) chromosome. Breeders and genetics researchers like Mendel had observed for a long time that offspring showed the effects of combined traits from both parents. Moreover, Morgan had hypothesized that very process. Now, McClintock believed, they could show physical proof of crossover by using hands-on cytological techniques. Once Creighton was finished, scientists would know much more about how crossovers worked.

The Experiment

The project had two parts. For the first part, they needed to find a set of markers—stainable, unique features—located on a chromosome that usually carried a set of linked genes. This setup would enable the two scientists to track the chromosome through the process of crossing-over. For the second part, they needed to find an easily observed set of genetic markers expressed in the phenotype on the same chromosome, so they could verify the simultaneous crossover movement of both the genes and the chromosomes. McClintock had already done some of the work. She had found a suitable group of linked genes and had established that they all were located on the same chromosome. All she needed now were two distinct markers near two distinct genes on that same chromosome. Once they had located and identified these elements, the two cytologists could follow the markers through the process of mating with a parent that did not have those markers on the counterpart chromosome. This would enable them to tell, according to cytological analysis, whether the chromosome crossover and gene crossovers were, in fact, the same event.

However, a lot of backbreaking fieldwork had to be done before they could even begin their cytological study under the microscope. Creighton began at the beginning that summer, with the corn kernels that showed the genetic and cytological markers that McClintock had observed. These kernels were the seeds from which their parent plants would grow. Failing to grow these seeds into strong, reproducing cornstalks would end the experiment before it began.

Maize Researchers at Work

Maize (scientifically known as *Zea mays*) is an ideal subject for genetic studies for several reasons. The variety of colors and patterns—known as variegation—that appear in maize kernels provide the equivalent of a full-color chart representing the genetic data, which are reflected in the kernels on the cob. In addition, maize can be either self-fertilized or cross-fertilized because each maize plant has both male and female flowers, bearing male flowers, or pollen, in the tassel and female flowers at the base of the silk. Self-fertilization is a useful option for the researcher, allowing for inbreeding that produces particularly pronounced extremes of genetic results.

Corn planted in the spring reaches sexual maturity in mid-July, so that became the peak work period for Cornell's maize geneticists, as they revved up and went into action. They spent every day (including weekends) in the cornfields from dawn to dusk working to control the mating so the experiments would be set up as planned.

In nature, wind and insects carry the pollen to neighboring silks. When a grain of pollen reaches a neighboring ear, it germinates, sending sperm through a long tube to an egg at the base of the cob. The sperm and egg cells (also called sex cells or germ cells) fuse and form a kernel. The embryo within the kernel will form the next generation. Each combination of sperm and egg produces one kernel.

However, in an experiment the researcher must control the variables and therefore pollination is not left to chance. To be sure that the right pollination gets to the right silks, geneticists cover the tassels and the ears with paper bags, preventing pollen from traveling and preventing ova from fusing with unwanted sperm. Then they transfer the pollen inside the bags to the silk by hand—taking pollen from a plant's own bag for self-fertilization.

At first Creighton did not realize the level of trust McClintock showed by placing the seeds in the younger scientist's care. Then she recognized they were doing something no one had ever done before. Here they were on the cutting edge of maize cytogenetics. Creighton spent many hot days in the cornfield, planting the precious kernels of corn in a shallow valley with a warm, southern exposure. From early daylight until nearly suppertime, she tended the plants. If they became sick or died, she would lose the whole summer's work, and the young plants needed irrigating and weeding. Other tasks also needed attention. The two researchers tagged sprouting plants to keep track of genetic history. They controlled pollination by covering the male tassels with paper bags to keep unwanted pollen from traveling to the female silks via gravity, wind, or insects. Finally, Creighton and McClintock pollinated by hand, using pollen carefully harvested from plants having the desired genetic history.

Typically, McClintock and Creighton ended each hot, physically demanding day in the maize field with a rousing game of tennis. Creighton was an excellent tennis player, but she later admitted that McClintock was as aggressive playing tennis as she was relentless pursuing chromosomes.

Creighton followed the routine that summer, but she did the work at first without real enthusiasm. Then, about halfway through the summer, she realized that she was literally tilling fresh ground that no one else had ever touched. Then she began to own the project and took pride in its importance. McClintock's enthusiasm was infectious, and Creighton found the challenges of working with this hardworking, energetic scientist invigorating.

Students and colleagues alike have remarked that McClintock was sometimes hard to understand, and she had little patience for those who did not manage to follow her explanations. No intellectual slouch herself, Creighton quickly came to recognize the key to keeping up with her mentor. When McClintock seemed to skip a beat, Creighton realized that she was in fact answering an unasked question—the one that her listeners should have asked but did not. Creighton learned to listen for jumps in McClintock's discourse and focus on the gaps to find the deeper questions between the lines. This insight gave Creighton a priceless key to communication—opening doors to understanding McClintock's complex cytological analyses and consistently meeting McClintock's high expectations.

Publishing the Results

The following summer, Thomas Hunt Morgan was the invited speaker at Cornell's prestigious Messenger Lectures, attended by students and faculty alike. After his last lecture, he took the opportunity to make the rounds, visiting his Cornell colleagues in their labs to talk shop.

When he stopped by to visit McClintock and Creighton, he listened with great interest as Creighton described their project. Had they submitted their results yet to a peer-reviewed journal? No, Creighton replied. Wanting to be certain, they were waiting for further results to be available from the 1931 crops before going public.

Publication is one of the principal drivers that turn the wheels of science—an engine that travels the path to fame and success for work done and discoveries made and the opportunity for other scientists to build on a colleague's work. The progress of science depends on this continual openness, the flow of knowledge it encourages, and the opportunity for correction and refinement. However, not every article submitted receives publication. Upon completion of any significant experiment and the analysis of its results, researchers may submit an account of their results to a journal in their field. Or if the interest is broad enough, they try one of the more general—and prestigious—scientific journals, such as *Science* or *Nature*. Submissions generally include an open account of their methods and results (whether or not they turn out as expected). If the journal's editor thinks the account would interest his or her readers, the article receives a review by one or more peers—other scientists in the same field—for a critique. If the account passes review, the editor may approve it for publication. When other scientists draw upon information in a published article or note, they provide a reference, or citation, to give credit to their sources. In this way, one's work becomes known, and as scientists participate in this constant and open interchange of information, they form a network of colleagues who learn from each other.

McClintock and Harriet Creighton remained friends throughout their lifetimes. Here they consult during a Cold Spring Harbor symposium in the 1950s. (Cold Spring Harbor Laboratory Archives)

Not everyone was as sure as Morgan was that the time had come for Creighton and McClintock to publish their results. The two researchers wanted the extra security that a second set of data would produce. Sharp, Creighton's adviser, was concerned because Creighton had not yet completed her Ph.D. The results from this experiment formed the basis for her doctoral dissertation, and she was still obligated to fulfill a three-year residency requirement before she would receive her degree. As Creighton recalled the event, Morgan pressed the point that delay could cause them to be scooped on a breakthrough that they obviously were the first to make. If they waited, someone else might get the credit for being first. She recalled that on the spot, Morgan penned a quick note to the editor of the *Proceedings of the National Academy of Sciences.* As a result of Morgan's urging, Creighton and McClintock submitted their account of the experiment in early July, and it was published shortly thereafter, in August. It is commonly referred to as Creighton and McClintock 1931, and it is widely accepted as one of biology's greatest experiments.

Tradition has it that Morgan later confessed that he knew at that time that Curt Stern, at the Kaiser Wilhelm Institute in Germany, was working on a similar experiment using fruit flies. Communication was slower then than it is now, and Stern did not find out about Creighton and McClintock 1931 until after he presented his own results with *Drosophila* at a meeting several months later. When asked about urging the two maize researchers to speed up their plans, Morgan said simply, "I thought it was about time that corn got a chance to beat *Drosophila!*" Stern had the advantage of new generations every 10 days, after all, whereas maize researchers had to wait a year for one set of results in the climate zone where they were working. And they were, without question, the first.

As Marcus Rhoades once remarked about McClintock, she seemed to have a "green thumb" when it came to generating important research results. "Everything she touches turns into something big!" he exclaimed. This experiment was the beginning of what would turn out to be a long series of significant discoveries for McClintock. She and Harriet Creighton had shown that chromosomes were the carriers for the genes responsible for producing observable physical traits. Their work also served to explain that the process of crossing over—the exchange of pieces of chromosomes—helps produce the remarkable diversity of forms found among living things.

This paper established McClintock's status as a scientist. In their 1955 book *Great Experiments in Biology,* authors Mordecai L. Gabriel and Seymour Fogel wrote, "Beyond any question, this is one of the truly great experiments of modern biology." Writing in *Classic Papers in Genetics* (1959), editor James A. Peters remarked, "This paper has been called a landmark in experimental genetics. It is more than that—it is a cornerstone."

On the Road

(1931–1936)

At the end of the spring term in 1931, Barbara McClintock had made a decision. The congenial cytology group was breaking up: George Beadle left for Caltech in 1930, where he had a National Research Council Fellowship for postgraduate work and where Harriet Creighton and Marcus Rhoades were still working on their Ph.D.'s in 1931, and at the same time McClintock began orchestrating her own departure from the instructorship she had held for four and one-half years at Cornell. Rhoades would accept a position as a geneticist for the U.S. Department of Agriculture (USDA) in 1935. By the end of 1934, Creighton had accepted a faculty teaching position at Connecticut College for Women (CCW), where she hoped to become an assistant professor, attain tenure, and perhaps eventually gain promotion to full professor. With the move to CCW, Creighton's primary obligations were teaching, but she continued to conduct research.

McClintock's decision to leave became firm when she received a two-year National Research Council (NRC) award. Obtaining a research fellowship was almost taken for granted for male recipients of a Ph.D., but for McClintock, as a woman scientist in the early 1930s, it was a great honor—one that McClintock saw as proof of her good luck (but was in fact more likely proof of recognized excellence in her work). In these bleak depression-era years, money was hard to get, too, and this fellowship made continued research possible. Frugal in her personal lifestyle and self-sufficient in her work,

Throughout her career, McClintock worked her own cornfield plot of several thousand plants, which she personally grew from her own seeds and pollinated for research. (Cold Spring Harbor Laboratory Archives)

she could make a small amount of money go a long way. For her, the future held a fulfilling two years of research at two of the most respected institutions in cytology and genetics—the University of Missouri, where she would work with Lewis Stadler; and Caltech, where she would work with E. G. Anderson (and where George Beadle and Charles Burnham went and where Thomas Hunt Morgan had moved from Columbia University in 1928).

McClintock bought an old Model A Ford roadster for criss-crossing the country as she traveled in nomadic style from one lab to another, using Cornell as her home base and traveling back and forth among the labs at Caltech, Missouri, and Cornell. When the old car broke down as it ate up miles and miles of dust, she hauled out her tools and repaired it herself. The summer months of 1931 took her to Missouri, where she worked with Lewis Stadler on X-ray irradiation. She spent the winter months of 1931–32, her first academic year as an NRC fellow, at Caltech, also returning to the west coast for the second winter, with visits in between to her home base at Cornell.

Overall this highly productive period was marked by a joyous freedom to excel. Through the fellowship, McClintock had funding, enabling all three venues to give her access to their best equipment and their finest geneticists—despite the financial shadow of the Great Depression, her fellowship relieved the institutions of any financial burden. She received warm invitations from both Stadler at the University of Missouri and E. G. Anderson at Caltech. Her work at Caltech, however, became threatened briefly because all such invitations required approval by the board of trustees even though there was no financial problem. McClintock was the first female postdoctoral fellow to be invited to the all-male school, and the trustees wavered at first but decided to allow her to come. On her first day, as she recalled it, she was taken to lunch at the faculty club, where postdoctoral fellows could become members. She recalled walking in the door and making her way toward a table. The room fell silent she later said. The usual buzz of conversation came to a dead stop, and McClintock became self-conscious under the obvious scrutiny. "What's wrong with me?" she asked. The news of the trustees' meeting was out, came the reply, and

At Caltech, McClintock often visited with chemist Linus Pauling years before he became a Nobel laureate in 1954. (The National Library of Medicine)

everyone was curious. After that day, McClintock recalled she never went back, and she kept to herself, venturing only as far as her own lab aside from visits with the famed biologist Linus Pauling, who was known to be a liberal on most issues and probably on the question of women's rights. McClintock had free access where it mattered, though, and she had many friends at Caltech, all of whom made her feel welcome, including the Morgans, in whose home she visited while working there. Caltech took another 40 years to hire the university's first woman professor.

X-rays in Missouri

The University of Missouri, like Cornell, is a land-grant college with links to the United States Department of Agriculture (USDA). The main campus was and is located in the small college town of Columbia in central Missouri, in a region known as "Little Dixie," where bitter Civil War struggles of the 1860s were not forgotten. The school was more structured than Cornell was, but McClintock had made friends with Missouri geneticist Lewis Stadler in 1926 when she was working on her doctorate at Cornell and he was a post-doctorate NRC fellow studying under Rollins Emerson. Stadler and McClintock had established a friendship and a lot of mutual respect during that time.

Stadler had been exposing maize pollen to X-ray radiation and studying the effects, a procedure he came up with independently in about 1926 at about the same time Hermann J. Muller began using X-rays to induce mutations in fruit flies. (Muller had scooped Stadler on this, though, publishing his results in 1927, a year earlier than Stadler. For this work, Muller received the 1947 Nobel Prize in physiology or medicine.) *Mutations* are accidental changes in the genes or chromosomes, and they are interesting for many reasons. They are the means by which an organism evolves, so of course they interest evolutionists, but geneticists trying to map the locations of genes on a chromosome had their own reasons for interest in mutations: A mutated gene is by definition different from the parent gene. So by breeding a mutated fruit fly, for example, with a "normal" specimen, researchers could track down what was happening during cell division—especially in crossover during meiosis.

Early genetic work with mutations had to just wait for them to happen—a very slow process, especially for maize plants with only one or two crops a year. However, by exposing maize pollen to X-rays, Stadler had shown he could hurry up the mutation process dramatically. Both the frequency of mutations and the variety of their manifestations were vastly more abundant. As a result, cytogeneticists like McClintock and Stadler had many more samples to probe, opening the gateways to understanding the structure and processes of genes and chromosomes.

McClintock was delighted to be part of this cutting-edge work, and she found both the process and its results greatly interesting. (In fact, her observations and studies of mutations in maize kernels would eventually lead to her greatest work, the discovery of transposable genetic elements, or "jumping genes," which has served as the cornerstone of the foundations of today's genetic engineering.)

To produce increased numbers of mutations quickly, Stadler collected pollen grains from plants that had dominant genes for traits he planned to study and exposed these pollen grains to X-rays. Then he selected kernels from plants having recessive genes for the same traits. He pollinated the flowers (silks) with the irradiated pollen (exposed to X-ray radiation). The results were dramatic. The radiation caused large-scale changes in the arrangements of the chromosomes in the offspring—resulting in easily discerned changes in the young plants. A wide variety of changes appeared in the offspring, but they were especially apparent in the coloring and textures of the kernels.

McClintock spent that summer identifying exactly what changes took place at the chromosome level. Here is where her ability to "get down" into the cell and look around proved priceless. The minute physical changes caused in the chromosome structure by exposure to the X-rays were difficult to find, but McClintock was able to spot them. The exchanges that took place between damaged and normal chromosomes during meiosis had produced a trail of broken pieces, missing or "lost" pieces, changed order (inversion), and transfers from a normal location often to a different chromosome altogether (translocation or transposition). McClintock was elated. She later remarked that much of what she had seen was exciting new territory. In December 1931, she published the results of her summer's work in the University of Missouri's Agricultural Experiment Station bulletin.

Ring Chromosomes

Sometimes McClintock had flashes of insight she could not explain— as often happens to people who have remarkable breadth and depth of knowledge in a subject, as well as keen expertise. Such was the

McClintock found that variegated color in maize stalks and leaves was caused by a mutation due to a loss of a ring chromosome. (The Barbara McClintock Papers, American Philosophical Society)

case with a group of variegated plants that she saw one day in the maize plots in Missouri. She recognized the variegation as a mutation caused by X-ray radiation, a mixing of dominant and recessive traits. She later recalled, "I didn't look at the variegated plants, but somehow or other they stuck in my mind."

That fall, in 1931, as she liked to tell the story, McClintock received a reprint sent to her by a researcher at the University of California at Berkeley, describing the same kind of variegation McClintock had seen in Missouri. The Berkeley researchers also mentioned a small chromosome, possibly broken off from or otherwise involved with a missing or "lost" fragment of genetic material.

The pieces seemed to fit together suddenly as in a jigsaw puzzle, McClintock later recalled, prompting her to think, "Oh this is a ring chromosome, because a ring chromosome would do this." Researchers had found ring chromosomes before, but no one had ever before known them to cause variegated coloring in plants. However, McClintock knew so well the kinds of knotting that sometimes occurred during crossing over and the changes that would occur in different situations during cell division that she could see it all happening as if she were watching it with her microscope.

The ring chromosome mutation usually forms when a chromosome breaks and the broken ends connect to each other. In this case, McClintock surmised that the chromosome carrying the dominant gene for color broke and formed a ring early in the plant's development. The ring would ordinarily be passed on in the normal fashion during cell division's dance of the chromosomes, and the normally dominant color would develop as usual. In this case, though, sometimes the ring did some fancy footwork instead. The footwork involved "sister strand exchanges" (chromatid exchanges) that produced two rings instead of one. The smaller ring contained no centromere (the structure at which the two arms of a chromosome normally attach). The other ring contained two centromeres. When the dominant color ended up on the smaller ring, it got "lost," producing plants with varied colorings, known as variegation. When she wrote back to the researcher about her thoughts, he wrote back, remarking, "It's a crazy idea, but it's the only one we've had."

As McClintock would recall later, the following summer, back in Missouri, McClintock strolled confidently through the field, pointing out variegated plants and telling Stadler her prediction, certain that a look through the microscope would bear out each one. At the same time, she was surprised at her own audacity, but back in the lab, the microscope did bear her out—from the very first slide all her predictions were correct.

Later that year, while out in California for a visit to Caltech during the 1932–33 academic year, she received an invitation from Susumu Ohno, a researcher, and his colleagues at UC Berkeley to visit their lab. When she arrived, she was ushered into a room where a microscope was set up on a table. She looked through the lens, and there it was—a ring chromosome. While no paper trail may exist to document this particular tale of triumph, it was a glorious story and McClintock enjoyed telling it.

When McClintock arrived in Missouri, Lewis Stadler had asked her to examine the chromosomes of his X-irradiated plants, and she had found that specific structural changes at the chromosome level had caused the predictable abnormalities observed in the plants. The structural changes she uncovered included translocation (transfer of part of a chromosome to a new location, sometimes on another chromosome—now more commonly known as transposition), inversions (breakage of a chromosome in two places and reinsertion in reverse orientation), deletions (in which sections of a chromosome are lost), ring chromosomes, and this last formation, the breakage-fusion-bridge.

In years to come, she would build on these studies, which formed the foundation of a lifetime body of work, as well as the tools for systematically teasing new understanding of genetics and heredity out of her maize stocks—and beyond to broader implications for other species of the biological world.

The Nucleolar Organizer Region

In the fall of 1933, McClintock spent her final term on the NRC fellowship at Caltech, where she turned her attention to chromosome 6—the chromosome that had an odd feature resembling an appended satellite, which actually was a dense nuclear structure known by this time as the *nucleolus*. (Researchers had not yet discovered much about the nucleolus at the time. There, messenger RNA accepts molecules of transfer RNA carrying amino acids, which are then assembled into proteins.)

On chromosome 6, she saw another interesting formation, located at the end of the chromosome, next to the point of attachment to the nucleolus. This minuscule mystery site had intrigued McClintock for quite awhile, although no one else seemed to share her interest. She became sure it had some role in the development of the nucleolus, and she called it the Nucleolar Organizer Region (NOR) because she saw that material apparently had to pass through the NOR, which somehow enabled it to become organized or structured as the nucleolus.

Geneticist A. E. Anderson at Caltech had some material he invited McClintock to look at, and she found some instances where a translocation had broken the NOR in two. In these cases, she observed that each part of the divided NOR could organize a separate nucleolus.

Cornell: A Brief Return

The NRC days were ending, and McClintock said good-bye to Beadle, Anderson, and the Morgans, and she returned to Cornell, where her good friend Dr. Esther Parker had made her home available to McClintock as a home base. Parker, a physician, had served during World War I as an ambulance driver and now practiced medicine in Ithaca.

McClintock's fellowship from the National Research Council concluded in 1933. These years had been remarkably fertile, with an amazing freedom to pursue her interests and work productively with the research giants of her field, including Thomas Hunt Morgan (University of California at Berkeley), Rollins A. Emerson (Cornell), and Lewis J. Stadler (University of Missouri). Every day of those years had been exciting and productive for McClintock—from the moment she got up, she was like a child opening gifts. "I couldn't wait to get to the laboratory in the morning, and I just hated sleeping."

Looking back years later in a speech before the American Association of University Women (AAUW), she described the importance she felt such an opportunity provided for a young scientist: "For the young person, fellowships are of the greatest importance. The freedom they allow for concentrated study and research cannot be duplicated by any other known method. They come at a time when one's energies are greatest and when one's courage and capacity to enter new fields and utilize new techniques are at their height."

As her funding came to an end, McClintock applied to the Guggenheim Foundation for another fellowship. Morgan, Emerson, and Stadler all wrote letters of recommendation, along with several other colleagues. She hoped to have the opportunity to work with Curt Stern at the Kaiser Wilhelm in Dahlem, and her work would be funded. All this sounded good. However, McClintock was unaware of the menacing turn politics in Germany had taken. She was not alone. Most of the American public had little information about what was happening in Germany in the 1930s.

Prewar Germany

When Barbara McClintock arrived in Germany, she was both alarmed and depressed by the ever-present storm troopers and the hate campaigns against the Jews. Curt Stern was no longer there, having decided to remain permanently in California, but she hit it off with Richard Goldschmidt, the current director of the Kaiser Wilhelm Institute for Biology. He was Jewish but apparently felt less vulnerable to persecution; he did recognize ominous warning signs, however, and left Germany for the University of California at Berkeley three years later. In writing about the early 1930s in his memoir, Goldschmidt remarked ironically, "It was not pleasant to return from a concert at night and to ride in the suburban train with a gang of storm troopers who were singing the beautiful song, 'If the Jew's blood drips from our knives, we feel happy, oh so happy.' But these things still were mere pinpricks compared with what was to come later after we had left."

A freewheeling thinker, Goldschmidt had an ego to match, and McClintock liked both characteristics. His thinking was unbound by scientific dogma and did not accept ideas just because they were

Exodus of Scientists: Germany in the 1930s

Following defeat at the end of World War I in 1918, the citizens of Germany went through some hard times. Inflation was rampant, and misery abounded. Many people were angry. To this provocative mix of emotions came a strange but charismatic young man who gave Germany back its sense of national pride and hope for the future. He also gave them someone to blame: the Jews, gypsies, and homosexuals—any non-Aryan or "unwanted" group, but especially the Jews, a large, often successful segment of the population that had long suffered persecution throughout the world. When the young man stirred the fires of envy and resentment among the depression-ridden populace, the strategy served to increase his popularity. Adolf Hitler became chancellor in 1933 and began to implement his plans for a rise to absolute power.

Already by 1933 Hitler had laid the groundwork for oppression and genocide. In 1925, the SS (*Schutzstaffel,* or "defense echelon") was founded as a special security force to form Hitler's personal bodyguard. This group attained increasingly broader powers in the years to come. Another group, the gestapo storm troopers (*Geheime Staatspolizei,* or "secret police"), was formed in 1933, the year of McClintock's arrival in Germany.

Persecution of the Jews began immediately. By February 1933, a decree gave the government the right to arrest individuals without cause. Jewish families, gypsies, homosexuals, suspected opponents of Hitler's Nazi party, and others considered to be a drain on Nazi power disappeared in the night, then were arrested and dragged off to concentration camps.

Many scientists, Jewish or not, began to leave their homes and careers in Germany as the Nazis began to remove Jewish researchers from official or administrative positions, at first, and later from their research and teaching positions. Included among those who fled Nazi-held countries in the 1930s were such luminaries as Albert Einstein (once director of the Kaiser Wilhelm Institute in Berlin), Max Born, Erwin Schrödinger, and Enrico Fermi. Curt Stern was in good company in making his decision not to return. By 1936, geneticist Richard B. Goldschmidt would also cross the Atlantic to a safer venue offered by the University of California at Berkeley.

Barbara McClintock walked right into the beginnings of the Holocaust, a reign of terror from 1933 to 1945, during which the Nazis executed 6 million people (a conservative estimate—some historians place the count much higher).

popular. He also was not afraid to be wrong, and he had a fertile mind. For example, he rejected Darwin's idea that evolution takes place gradually. Instead he maintained that new species result from sudden, big genetic changes that he called "macromutations." "I approved of his way of thinking. I approved of his freedom," McClintock once remarked. As always, McClintock saw freedom as the healthiest approach to both science and life.

Goldschmidt understood McClintock's discomfort and suggested she go to Freiburg, away from most of the political activity, to work with Friedrich Oehlkers, a developmental geneticist whose specialty was studies of environmental influences on germ cell formation.

Working with the Lion

Despite her depression, McClintock kept working while in Freiburg, writing a paper on her observations regarding the nucleolus. This mysterious and intriguing rounded feature of a cell's nucleus was little understood at the time, but McClintock's paper did not come together well. She later admitted it was badly written, although it was published in *Zeitschrift fur Zellforschung und mikroskopische Anatomie,* a respected German journal, in 1934 and became a classic paper known as "The Relation of a Particular Chromosomal Element to the Development of the Nucleoli in *Zea mays.*"

Noting that "Germany devastated McClintock," science historian Nathaniel Comfort points out that readers may rightly attribute this paper's lack of clarity and inconsistent use of terms to McClintock's state of mind when she wrote it. However, he also hints that she may have been influenced by embryologist Hans Spemann, whom Comfort characterizes as the "lion of Freiburg." Recipient of the Nobel Prize in physiology or medicine in 1935, Spemann leaned philosophically toward vitalism, a doctrine generally discredited among scientists that maintains that a nonmaterialistic force or energy provides the life and functions of a living organism.

Earlier in his career, from 1901 to 1906, Spemann worked on a process he called embryological induction. In this process, one tissue induces, or causes, the formation of a new kind of tissue by contact with it. Later, in the 1920s, he came up with a concept known as the "organizer." This was a special tissue that caused induction of the neural plate, a primordial tissue of the nervous system. However, this action was not caused by naturalistic processes in Spemann's view. Instead of producing its effect by secreting chemicals, the organizer tissue created a "field," he believed, acting as a vitalistic agent, a sort of master planner, instructing and organizing the tissue it contacted. Despite this metaphysical inclination, however, Spemann made many contributions to the understanding of embryonic development, and his findings on organizers had a broad influence on the field of developmental biology. It is not surprising that McClintock worked on her own organizer concept—the Nucleolar Organizer Region (NOR)—while working at Spemann's institution.

Despondent and withdrawn, McClintock did not stay the full term of her fellowship. She returned home to Ithaca and Cornell in 1934. The Guggenheim Foundation extended her stipend to fill out the original time span, and she used it to continue her work at Cornell. When that ran out, Emerson persuaded the Rockefeller Foundation to grant a two-year fellowship of $1,800 a year to provide Emerson with an assistant, which was actually just another way to provide McClintock a stopgap income so she could continue her research. All this helped for the moment, but the lack of a clear path and a permanent appointment began to wear on her.

5

The Missouri Years
(1936–1941)

Barbara McClintock had been widely acclaimed for her research, and she had produced a solid body of publications, yet she felt frustrated. Her job prospects were nil, and she was at loose ends. Funding for her Rockefeller award was ending at Cornell, and even though Ithaca always felt like home, McClintock saw that the path she was traveling was a dead end. Spring had arrived, and she was going nowhere. "No sign of a job has turned up for me as yet," she wrote to a friend in April 1935. She complained of low spirits and a disturbing sense of uncertainty. Her work suffered, she said; she felt she needed the freedom to "just work," with a sense of security.

In the spring of 1936, another possibility turned up in Missouri, and the horizon seemed to brighten. Lewis Stadler offered McClintock a faculty position as an assistant professor at the University of Missouri at Columbia. This appointment would give

While working with Lewis Stadler at the University of Missouri, McClintock did much of the groundwork for her most important discoveries. (University Archives, University of Missouri at Columbia, L. J. Stadler, 1938, C: 1/141/7 Box 1)

her an opportunity to return to the X-ray research she had worked on with Stadler in the summers of 1931 and 1932 as an NRC fellow.

McClintock felt, however, that the position did not really offer the security for which she had hoped. Despite the ranking at a step above instructors on the faculty scale, she felt the title of assistant professor did not give her either an adequate salary increase or recognition of her stature. However, it was a firm offer, including a promise of tenure, historian Lee Kass points out, after 10 years of service. She had always gotten on well with Stadler, and the mid-Missouri campus was familiar territory from her NRC postdoctoral days, so she accepted.

The Breakage-Fusion-Bridge Cycle

In examining the chromosomes that Stadler had irradiated, McClintock found a kind of frayed-end breakage in the chromosomes exposed to the X-rays. Remarkably, these frayed ends seemed to mend themselves by fusing with the frayed ends of other broken chromosomes. Then, during later cell division, the process may place so much stress on these patched areas that they break again. Each time the mended area of the chromosome breaks, it loses more genetic information. McClintock named this process using the hyphenated name of its three steps—the breakage-fusion-bridge cycle.

McClintock's publication of her description of this cycle in 1938 prompted praise from her community of colleagues. It confirmed her status as a star, as one of the giants of maize cytology. The breakage-fusion-bridge cycle not only stood as one of McClintock's masterly observations, but it also became a highly useful new tool for deep exploration of the chromosome.

McClintock was rhapsodic about the discovery. "Have been working like hell on an exciting over-all problem in genetics with wonderful results," she exclaimed in a note to a colleague in 1940. "It gets me up early and puts me to bed late!"

Instead of seeing these observations only in terms of the way particular types of chromosome breakage play out in maize plants, McClintock cast a wider net, and she caught sight of some bigger implications—not just for the study of maize but also for heredity in other life-forms. She saw that when the frayed ends of broken chromosomes seemed to find each other and fuse together, these tiny structures were actually mending themselves. How did the frayed ends of these broken chromosomes find each other? How did they know how to repair themselves? This kind of emergency repair—calling for an ad hoc strategy—spoke to McClintock of bigger capabilities than genes previously were thought to have. "The conclusion seems inescapable," she wrote, "that cells are able to sense the presence in their nuclei of ruptured ends of chromosomes and then to activate a mechanism that will bring together and then unite these ends, one with another. . . . The ability of a cell to sense these broken ends, to direct them toward each other, and then to unite them so that the union of two DNA strands is correctly oriented is a particularly revealing example of the sensitivity of cells to all that is going on within them."

McClintock would later conclude that the BFB cycle uncovered the breakage mechanism, but this insight had not come to her yet. Ultimately, she would shape a new view of the chromosome that defied the accepted picture of stable genes strung along a chromosome like pearls on a necklace. McClintock would soon begin to envision an overhaul of the concept of the genetic process, one that involved signals being sent and received from both inside and outside the cell, interpretations being made, and information processed. These concepts put McClintock at least 15 years ahead of her time.

In Search of a Position

Despite the progress McClintock was making with her research, however, by the summer of 1940 she became severely frustrated and anxious. She had received no hint of an offer of advancement at the University of Missouri, despite continuing recognition from the outside world. In 1939, she was elected vice president of the Genetics Society of America—a clear recognition of her stature. The following year she would be president. She continued to publish actively, with five papers of which she was the sole author published between 1937 and 1939 and three more in 1941, also authored solely by McClintock.

McClintock began to have a foreboding sense that no offer would ever be made. Advancement to associate professor would be a commitment from the university to award a full professorship within a few years and with it full tenure.

The entire decade of the 1930s reflected hard times—nearly everyone suffered during the Great Depression ushered in by the 1929 stock market crash at the beginning of the decade. Jobs were scarce, and economic security was rare. Also, by the late 1930s and early 1940s, the specter of war hung in the air. McClintock faced the additional unjust problem that universities were notorious for rarely offering the honor and security of tenure to a woman, and the University of Missouri was no exception.

McClintock also recognized that in hard times pure research positions were generally the first to be eliminated. A teacher helped attract and educate students who supported the university with their tuition payments. She worried that, instead of being attractive to the university because of her research contributions, she thought she actually was more vulnerable, even though she was willing to teach, and did.

Considerable friction existed between McClintock and Mary Jane Guthrie, who was already on the faculty when McClintock arrived and since then had received an appointment as an associate professor. With as strong a personality as McClintock, Guthrie was known to become jealous about her territory and to make life pointedly miserable for those she considered to be in her way. She clearly considered McClintock to be in her way.

McClintock believed that others whose credentials were less impressive had been hired as additions to the faculty at the associate professor level, while McClintock was still assistant professor after five years. Finally, she went to the dean to ask, "What are my chances here?" The dean replied, she told Keller, that if Stadler left, McClintock would probably be fired. McClintock had a reputation for being "difficult" and "troublesome," and by the time she visited the dean, she was probably angry and may have provoked the heated retort. In any case, the relationship had been deteriorating for a long time—and from the beginning, her position had depended on Stadler.

Stadler had a lot of clout with the university—he had brought an $80,000 Rockefeller Foundation grant to Missouri and was spearheading the growth of a major genetics center. His affiliation, strictly speaking, was with the U.S. Department of Agriculture (USDA) Field Station in Columbia, but the two institutions were hooked together, so when he decided he wanted McClintock's prestige and capabilities on board, he got what he wanted. (The win was no doubt all the easier considering that McClintock's salary came out of his grant money.) She also surmised that announcements of faculty openings at other schools apparently had been intercepted by the department and never delivered to her, although this conclusion may be questionable. (If people wanted her to leave, what motive would they have for intervening in this way?)

Looking back, McClintock said she recognized that the University of Missouri was never a good fit for her. She recalled one time she turned up at her lab on the weekend without her keys. Without ever thinking what "people might think," she pulled herself up to the sill, opened the window, and slid in. She was the talk of the campus—someone even caught the "unladylike" act on film. But the woman who wore knickers playing ball games as a kid in the streets of Brooklyn (and who by this time wore pants nearly all the time) thought that climbing in the laboratory window was just practical and an obvious solution to a pesky problem.

McClintock irked the administration by counseling graduate students to change schools if she thought they would be better off elsewhere. Moreover, she often arrived in Columbia late for the start of the school year—which probably seemed all right to her, since her NRC days had established a precedent of working under a free rein, and especially since, Kass reports, she had permission from the department chair—but overall she projected the image of a renegade.

Moving On

By 1941, according to Kass, McClintock had announced her decision to Stadler. In correspondence with her old friend Marcus Rhoades in October of that year, Stadler expressed his belief that Missouri was about to grant a promotion, and the university did make her an offer, but by then it was too little too late. She visited Rhoades that summer at Columbia University in New York, where he was then a professor. Rhoades said he would gladly share his research plot for the summer session at the Department of Genetics of the Carnegie Institute of Washington, D.C. at Cold Spring Harbor, Long Island, New York. By December, *Drosophila* expert Milislav Demerec, as acting director of Cold Spring Harbor, offered McClintock a temporary position at the Carnegie Institute's Department of Genetics. The appointment was soon extended, and Cold Spring Harbor became her permanent home in January 1943.

6

Cold Spring Harbor:
A Place to Work

(1942–1992)

Originally founded as a fish hatchery in 1880 by the Brooklyn Institute of Arts and Sciences, Cold Spring Harbor on Long Island in New York had redefined its purpose by 1890, when it became a biology laboratory designed to prove or disprove Charles Darwin's theory of evolution. In 1904, the year-round laboratories were funded by the Carnegie Institution of Washington as the Station for Experimental Evolution, later designated as the Department of Genetics. It was one of the earliest genetics research centers in the United States, and although other laboratories (including Morgan's lab at Columbia) soon overshadowed it as the top genetics lab in the country, Cold Spring Harbor continues to be recognized for its contributions to the field.

By the 1940s, when Rhoades and McClintock turned up there, Cold Spring Harbor's constellation of biological laboratories came

When McClintock arrived at the Carnegie Institution of Washington's Department of Genetics located at Cold Spring Harbor in December 1941, she found it a quiet and peaceful place to work, a sort of rustic camp for biological research, much as shown in this photograph from the 1950s. (The Barbara McClintock Papers, American Philosophical Society)

to life each summer as a sort of intensive camp for zoologists, marine life specialists, geneticists, botanists from all over—the whole gamut of life scientists gathering there during the summer months like wild creatures at a watering hole. They went there to work when the university laboratories slowed down, to study, to report and listen, to attend the summer seminars that burst the seams of the modest buildings. In winter, only a few people remained after the exodus back to research and teaching positions all over the world. Barbara McClintock arrived at the Cold Spring Harbor Laboratory complex in December 1941, where, except for lectures and short-term appointments, she remained for the rest of her life. Compared to university life or big laboratory settings, it was a peaceful place with few interruptions in the work day—an ideal setting for focused, productive research. It was an ideal home for McClintock and her work.

Continuing the Work

McClintock had an experimental plot near the water, where she planted her maize and meticulously controlled her crosses of different strains, continuing the work on broken chromosomes she had begun in Missouri.

In the spring of 1944, McClintock was elected to membership in the National Academy of Sciences, the most prestigious scientific organization in the United States. She was the third woman ever to be elected to the National Academy, and she became a member at the unusually young age of 41. At this point, McClintock began to recognize she was a model for other women who wanted to become scientists or to excel or to enter other professions that were dominated by men. "I knew then I was caught," she later reflected. "You see, I had all this freedom. Now I figured I couldn't let the women down." Now also, she would

Widely known as a wizard with a microscope, McClintock seemed to have unusually keen perception, augmented by insightful interpretation. (The Barbara McClintock Papers, American Philosophical Society)

not be able to flee to another profession. She would have to stay the course.

Another important event grew out of the election to the academy. George Beadle was also elected to membership that year (and was also young for the honor). Beadle had written to McClintock earlier in the year to ask if she would be willing to visit his lab at Stanford University in Palo Alto, California. He was working with *Neurospora,* a red bread mold, and because the chromosomes are so small, he and his colleagues were having difficulty with cytological analysis—the sort of thing that McClintock did so exceptionally well.

As McClintock enjoyed telling the story to Evelyn Keller, she was delighted to accept the invitation, and they settled on a date in October. McClintock arrived and settled in with her microscope. Everyone expected the usual McClintock "magic," but suddenly, for no apparent reason, McClintock was not so sure. After two days sitting at the microscope with no results, she was even less certain she could succeed. "I got very discouraged, and realized there was something wrong—something quite seriously wrong. I wasn't seeing things, I wasn't integrating, I wasn't getting things right at all. I was lost." So she got up, went outside, followed a path to a eucalyptus grove, sat down on a bench, and began to think. Later she confessed that she had shed a few tears in those moments of panic. A period, she said, of "very intense, subconscious thinking" followed. "And suddenly I knew everything would be just fine." She returned to the lab, her usual confidence back in charge. She had been gone just thirty minutes. Five days later, she had solved the puzzle, and two days after that she made her presentation. Not only had she found a count of seven for the chromosomes as she had done for maize, but she had also tracked each one through the process of meiosis. Since no one had yet succeeded in describing the meiotic process in fungi, this was a big step.

"Barbara, in two months in Stanford," Beadle later told a colleague, "did more to clean up the cytology of *Neurospora* than all other cytological geneticists had done in all previous time on all forms of mold."

The time spent thinking on the bench beneath the tall eucalyptus trees, she believed, was the key. She had taken time to reorient

Former Cornell postdoctorate and future Nobel laureate (1958) George Wells Beadle (1903–89) invited McClintock to Stanford University to help with identifying Neurospora chromosomes. (California Institute of Technology)

herself so she could absorb what she saw and process it, or integrate it, very rapidly, so that even though she was working with slides she could visualize a continuous process. Although this process sounds like magic, sitting down and "thinking hard," as Nobel physicist

Molecular Biology: A Powerful Approach

Like the particle physicists in the physical sciences, life scientists came into the second half of the 20th century with a mission: to study the smallest, most basic building blocks in their field, the architects of life. Out of this goal a new field was born: molecular biology, a melding of biochemistry and physics. This powerful new approach—the study of biology at the molecular level—deals with the characteristics and processes of the biological world as seen at the level of large organic molecules known as macromolecules. Unimaginable when Gregor Mendel labored in his garden before the beginning of the 20th century, the power and deep insight of the molecular-level discoveries of the 1940s to 1960s galvanized the science of genetics.

Early hints of the molecular revolution came from Friedrich Miescher (1844–95), who observed the presence of nucleic acids in cell nuclei in 1869, and in the 1880s, from Walther Fleming (1843–1905), who discovered chromosomes. Still, at first no one realized that any connection with heredity existed. Not until Thomas Hunt Morgan, filled with skepticism, began his now-familiar breeding experiments with fruit flies in 1907 did the study of heredity and its tiny, powerful mechanisms begin to take off. By 1911, his laboratory team at Columbia University succeeded in showing that the chromosome carried the agents of heredity, and in 1916, Calvin B. Bridges nailed down the proof for the chromosome theory.

In 1909, Phoebus Aaron Theodor Levene (1869–1940) became the first to find that nucleic acids contain a sugar named ribose, and 20 years later, he found that other nucleic acids contain another sugar, deoxyribose. These discoveries established that there are two types of nucleic acids: ribonucleic acid (RNA) and deoxyribo-

Richard Feynman used to say, is a key weapon in the arsenals of many brilliant scientists and other creative thinkers. This deep thinking gives the mind the time to bring to bear on a problem all the thinker's breadth of knowledge and experience, at the same time often changing the paradigm of approach. That is why McClintock knew she could overcome the difficulties she was having with seeing with the light microscope. Based on knowledge and experience

nucleic acid (DNA)—further prodding researchers' interest in the chemical nature of these complex substances.

Almost no one suspected that DNA was connected with heredity. Chromosomes were clearly involved and DNA existed in chromosomes, but so did proteins, which seemed so much more complex than DNA that they became the favored candidates for the job of carrying hereditary material—at least until Canadian-born American bacteriologist Oswald Avery (1877–1955) showed that the agent charged with carrying the genetic material of life is DNA, not proteins. Working in the early 1940s, Avery and Rockefeller Institute colleagues Maclyn McCarty (1911–2005) and Colin Macleod (1909–72) established that life-forms employ two categories of chemicals, one that stores information and a second that acts, based upon that information, to duplicate the organism. All indications pointed to the fact that enzymes carried out the instructions and DNA held the blueprints, which it also passed on in a nearly exact duplicate to the next generation.

In the early 1940s, while working with *enzymes* (specialized proteins that control the speed of biochemical reactions), McClintock's good friend George Beadle and his colleague Edward L. Tatum (1909–75) uncovered the "one gene/one enzyme" connection when they found that mutations in a gene resulted in defective enzymes. (One gene/one enzyme is the idea that each gene determines the structure of a particular enzyme, which in turn controls a single chemical reaction.) They concluded that genes were the regulators for all biochemical processes.

Even though a major piece of the puzzle remained unsolved—the structure of DNA—the field of molecular biology by this time had already proven its great potential as a tool for geneticists.

coupled with a new way to see that fit, she knew the new approach was right.

The Jumping Gene

Beginning in 1944, McClintock also began the work for which she is best known, flowing out of her studies of breakage in chromosomes,

Maize Kernels and the Jumping Gene

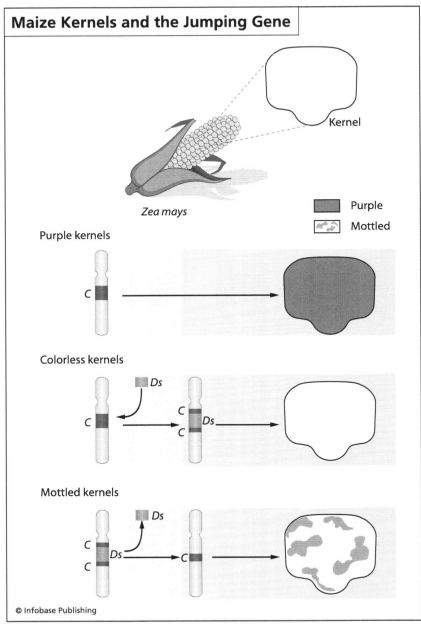

When McClintock first discovered jumping genes, she found that other scientists were skeptical that genes could move around like this and doubted that they had any controlling function. Finally, corroborating evidence was found. Since then, jumping genes, now known as transposable elements, have been found in many organisms, including bacteria and humans.

including her work on ring chromosomes and the breakage-fusion-bridge cycle. As she worked on her emerging theory, she recognized that she was cutting against the grain, but from the outset, she sensed that the evidence led in the direction she was testing. She persevered, even though for two years she was in limbo, not knowing whether the line of thought she was pursuing would pay off or wind up on the scrap heap.

During this time, McClintock made the acquaintance of Evelyn Witkin, a graduate student in bacterial genetics on fellowship at Cold Spring Harbor who was working in the same building and came by daily to visit. The two developed a mentor-student relationship, with McClintock frequently expounding on her current progress and problems. According to Keller, McClintock told Witkin that, despite a sense of working somewhat speculatively, she had confidence:

> It never occurred to me that there was going to be any stumbling block. Not that I had the answer, but [I had] the joy of going at it. When you have that joy, you do the right experiments. You let the material tell you where to go, and it tells you at every step what the next has to be because you're integrating with an overall brand new pattern in mind. You're not following an old one; you are convinced of a new one, and you let everything you do focus on that. You can't help it, because it all integrates. There were no difficulties.

Although McClintock's vocabulary may seem mystical, she was far too rigorous a scientist to rely on the reading of tea leaves. What she meant to evoke here was the sort of hunch that all productive scientists play on—based on her many years of close observation of the organism she was working with and her enormous skill at reading patterns and integrating hundreds of discrete observations.

The mechanism she proposed was a complex process of regulation and control that, at the time, was unlike anything yet observed. She saw that a control mechanism associated with a gene could cause a chromosome to break, dissociate, and rejoin differently—all in systematic, observable, and predictable ways. She arrived at this conclusion, as usual, by observing changes in color patterns in kernels of maize and correlating them with changes she observed in the chromosome structure.

Jumping Gene, A Closer Look

10
9
8
7
6
5
4
3
2
1

Ds

McClintock observed that some genetic material not only moves but also serves as a controlling element, or switch, that can turn other genes on and off. This diagram shows the control element that McClintock called Ds jumping from its original inactive place between two genes (8 and 9) to a place in the neighborhood of gene 4. When that happens, gene 4 "turns off"—that is, it temporarily stops production of its associated protein. Gene 4 switches back on, and synthesis of the protein resumes if Ds changes position again.

This part of McClintock's story began with some kernels of hybrid corn in which she noticed patches of color that differed in size. She suspected these strange patches of color were produced by what she called "mutable genes," that is, genes that seemed to lose and then regain their function. She wondered how that worked. Setting aside all other projects, McClintock focused on tracking down what was going on with these genes. The answers to her questions did not come easily. She spent two years just to complete the first step, which established that a section of chromosome was able to break away from the rest of the chromosome and insert itself in another place on the same chromosome. This action, she was able to prove, was caused by a gene, which in turn was activated by another gene some distance away on the chromosome. The controlling gene she called the activator (Ac). This was a rather startling statement— to assert that one part of the genome controlled another part. In 1946, the idea that a gene might reorganize one or more other genes under the direction of a controlling gene was a bit revolutionary but not entirely unexpected.

Next, McClintock studied dissociation for several years, along with the activator genes for each action. By 1948, she could show that both the dissociated chromosome section (Ds) and the activator (Ac) moved to another location after the controlled event. She gave the name "transposition" to this entire orchestration of events.

Through further testing and careful thought, within a year later (1949) she began to understand how this whole process became reflected in visible traits in the plants—for example, in the strangely shaped colored areas on a batch of hybrid kernels. She saw also how great an effect this programmed process could have on an individual plant. Ultimately, she came to realize that the random patterns of red and yellow kernels were controlled by a transposon, or "jumping gene" as it came to be called. (McClintock did not use the term *transposon*—drawn from the bacterial genetics literature—instead, she called the genes "controlling elements," a term that is no longer used.)

7

Presenting the Evidence

(1951–1956)

Barbara McClintock was most comfortable working in her fields of maize and gazing through the microscope in her lab, but she was no stranger to the lectern. In 1951, she was 49, a veteran speaker and an internationally recognized cytogeneticist. At the time of her presentation at the Cold Spring Harbor Symposium of 1951, however, she addressed her audience of fellow scientists with apprehension bordering on dread, as she recalled the event years later in an interview with biographer Evelyn Fox Keller. She knew her results were too complex to allow for clear discussion in the mere 60 minutes allotted in the conference schedule. She also knew some fellow scientists thought her approach was old-fashioned and out of date. She predicted to herself that they would think she was out of her mind. All these thoughts clamored at the back of McClintock's mind as she presented her research results.

In this photo taken at the 1951 Cold Spring Harbor Symposia on Quantitative Biology, McClintock appears to be in good spirits and fully confident, but she later recalled this meeting as a dismal and disheartening point in her career. Biographer Nathaniel Comfort concludes that her colleagues' reactions may not have been as negative as her later recollections indicated. (Cold Spring Harbor Laboratory Archives)

Finally, she reached the end of her remarks. What happened then is somewhat controversial. Everyone seems to agree that no one posed any questions at the time, and McClintock later clearly interpreted that reaction as a rejection. Was there a hush that reverberated throughout the room—a "stony silence," as Keller put it? Or was it, as some attendees suggested, a respectful silence? Photographs taken at the 1951 symposium show

McClintock deep in animated conversations with other scientists, not looking at all devastated or even tense. Much of her support system was there, including Harriet Creighton and Evelyn Witkin, and McClintock can be seen talking, laughing, and listening. She certainly did not seem to be struggling against a sense of rejection and depression.

Yet when she recollected the occasion later, McClintock recalled a dark time in her career. To be sure, it was the beginning of a long-term discomfort between McClintock and many other botanists, as well as molecular biologists, and a gnawing sense that she had lost much of the consistently positive peer respect that she had always enjoyed. According to McClintock, this time the reactions ranged from high skepticism from many and from some, a confused refusal even to listen.

On the other side, when the word got around to colleagues who were not there, Alfred Sturtevant, a highly respected geneticist from T. H. Morgan's team, announced with apparent certainty: "I didn't understand one word she said, but if she says it is so, it must be so!" Probably apocryphal, the story still offsets some of the sting of less enthusiastic reactions—at least those McClintock recalled. It also served to illustrate the intellectual respect McClintock commanded and the high degree of complexity of her work. For many reasons, fellow researchers saw McClintock's ideas about transposition as radical. They did not doubt her data but they thought that she was trying to generalize too much, that she was reading too much significance into her results—claiming universality for traits they thought might be limited to plants.

Skeptical Peers

In his book *The Tangled Field: Barbara McClintock's Search for the Patterns of Genetic Control,* science historian Nathaniel C. Comfort made a case that many of McClintock's colleagues accepted her research results but not her interpretation of her data. Comfort pointed out that McClintock would not have received an invitation to present her paper in the first place without a conviction among her peers that her ideas were worthwhile. Called "less than complete as a biography" by science historian Carla C. Keirns in a review for *American Scientist,* Comfort's book also received praise from the same reviewer as "the definitive work on Barbara McClintock's discovery of transposition," as well as her ambition to use controlling elements to explain development.

McClintock argued that some of her colleagues were too attached to the concept that genes were positioned immovably on a chromosome like so many pearls strung on a necklace. Clinging to immovability as a given, they assumed that if maize genes functioned differently, then the genetic makeup of maize must be unique, different from other species.

In addition, McClintock's arguments were complex and difficult to follow—partly because of the inherent complexity of maize genetics and partly because of McClintock's style. In James A. Peters's *Classic Papers in Genetics,* the editor saw the need to include this warning in the introduction of the 1931 paper that McClintock wrote with Harriet Creighton:

> It is not an easy paper to follow, for the items that require retention throughout the analysis are many, and it is fatal to one's understanding to lose track of any of them. Mastery of this paper, however, can give one the strong feeling of being able to master almost anything else he might have to wrestle with in biology.

By the 1950s, some, though not all, geneticists had turned away from maize as a subject for study. Many geneticists were working with either bacteria or bacteriophages (often called phages), viruses that infect bacteria and may insert themselves into the host cell. These tiny creatures had gained popularity because they are simple, easy to study, and incredibly fast at reproduction, with a new generation several times a day. They were the harbingers of the age of microbiology, and most microbiologists had little patience for the slow, complex maize plant or any other large, cumbersome organism. Molecular biology also was growing strong, and James Watson and Francis Crick's discovery in 1953 of the structure of the DNA molecule caused an enormous explosion of new discoveries. The excitement tended to overshadow the more plebian and seemingly obscure news about the role of controlling elements in maize.

DNA: The Double Helix (1953)

American biochemist James D. Watson was a whiz kid—when he was 12 he had been a contestant on a radio show called *Quiz Kids,* and he entered the University of Chicago as a freshman at the age of 15, graduating four years later with two bachelor's degrees, in philosophy and science. He was quick on his feet, sharp, and sassy, and he had always wanted to do something that would make him "famous in science." As a graduate student, he studied at the University of Indiana under Salvador E. Luria and Max Delbrück as well as geneticist Hermann Muller (who irradiated *Drosophila* with X-rays, thereby "scooping maize," as Morgan once put it, in reverse, in reference to Creighton/McClintock 1931). On travel as a postgraduate fellowship in Copenhagen, he met Maurice Wilkins, a biophysicist at King's College in London who was working on X-ray crystallography of DNA. Watson was fascinated by this idea of using a common method of chemical and physical analysis on a biological substance such as DNA. Just a few days later, he learned that biochemist Linus Pauling had discovered the structure of proteins was a helix—coiled like a notebook wire or a spring. Watson thought the two concepts—an innovative analysis technique and a structural model for a cousin molecule—might offer a place to start on the structure of DNA. He knew that the DNA molecule, often called the architect of life, provides the genetic blueprint for each cell, controlling every characteristic of a living organism. Its structure was a fundamental unknown, and scientists were racing to discover this key to understanding how genetics works.

So Watson took a detour, intending to go to London to learn more about DNA, but winding up instead at Cambridge. There he met British biophysicist Francis Crick, who was 12 years older than Watson and had a background in physics and chemistry and experience analyzing hemoglobin using X-ray crystallography. They

(continues on next page)

(continued from previous page)

hit it off immediately and were soon talking nonstop. It was the beginning of a great scientific collaboration.

In 1953, James Watson and Francis Crick succeeded in solving the mystery—helped immeasurably by X-ray diffraction pictures of the DNA molecule taken by British biophysicist Maurice Wilkins and British physical chemist Rosalind Franklin and by information supplied by Wilkins without Franklin's knowledge and despite an adversarial relationship with Franklin. Crick and Watson's model portrayed the structure of the DNA molecule as a double helix, with two parallel threads spiraling side by side and connected by a nearly endless ladder of cross bars—like a long spiral staircase having many steps. The rails of the staircase, they surmised, were composed of sugar phosphate, while the steps were

American biologist James Watson and British biophysicist Francis Crick teamed up at Cambridge University, hoping to discover the structure of DNA, which they did with the help of British chemist and X-ray diffraction specialist Rosalind Franklin and her colleague British biophysicist Maurice Wilkins. (Cold Spring Harbor Laboratory Archives)

McClintock made another presentation at the Cold Spring Harbor Symposium in 1953 and a third in 1956 without any greater success in connecting with most of her audience.

Persistence and Knowing: Return to Work

McClintock was deeply disappointed. She had carefully observed and probingly experimented. She had, as always, set up her experi-

composed of four bases—cytosine, guanine, adenine, and thymine—arranged in specific patterns and joined by hydrogen bonds. It was an enormous breakthrough.

In 1962, Crick, Watson, and Wilkins received the Nobel Prize for their pioneering work on the structure of the DNA molecule. (Franklin's premature death in 1958 of ovarian cancer barred her from candidacy because the Nobel is awarded only to living candidates. Would she have shared the 1962 Nobel Prize if she had lived longer? The answer will never be known.)

This landmark discovery of DNA's molecular structure encouraged the increasing acceptance of molecular biology as the key to understanding genetic processes—while cytogenetics became a less popular approach, considered old-fashioned by many geneticists, especially the younger ones.

Rosalind Franklin (1920–58) came close to solving the DNA structural puzzle between 1951 and 1953, but Crick and Watson beat her to it—with the help of her X-ray diffractions. Tragically, she died of cancer before the Nobel laureates were named. (Cold Spring Harbor Laboratory Archives)

ments flawlessly, planning her crossbreeding based on her painstaking documentation. She labeled and stored her stocks, knowing that her venture required accuracy in every aspect. "I knew there must be no mistake," she once told her friend biologist Howard Green, and she knew she had a well-earned reputation for flawless technique and ironclad organization. She also knew her colleagues trusted her honesty and care. She also had absolute confidence in the thought processes she had used to arrive at her conclusions and she received many citations of her work in the maize journals. Yet her colleagues (including Beadle) did not follow her, or could not understand her and citations in the molecular biology journals were few. Everyone thrives on positive reinforcement, of course, and the lack of it is painful and depressing—all the more difficult to take because she could see no reason for this reaction.

Yet, despite the sense of loss, she still had everything she needed most. She still had her work and the freedom to pursue this or any other project she envisioned. She still had her position, her lab, and her cornfields at Cold Spring Harbor. The Carnegie Institution always stood behind her and never wavered. She had no teaching duties or other obligations, no demands for research plans. McClintock always liked to develop her research paths as she went, ready to follow the unexpected trail that might pay off with some new result. Carnegie never stepped in with demands. From 1941 to 1967, she was a staff member of the Carnegie Institution of Washington's Genetics Department at Cold Spring Harbor, and after that, for the rest of her life until 1992, she served as distinguished service member. She was always grateful, from beginning to end, for the support she received from the Carnegie Institution and Cold Spring Harbor. McClintock would later remark, "If I had been some other place, I'm sure that I would've been fired for what I was doing because nobody was accepting it."

She continued to do her work—she could and did lose herself and her sorrow in the everyday joy of continuing to find out how things worked. In his essay "In Memoriam—Barbara McClintock," Howard Green wrote: "Barbara did not permit her inner disturbances to unsettle the course of her life or her work. This was possible only because she was so permeated by sincerity. Her accomplishments in science depended on her respect for the way things were and not on her need to discover something."

Sojourn in Latin America: The Origins of Maize

During these same years, McClintock became drawn into a search for the evolutionary trail of maize as a domesticated crop in Latin

America—and, ultimately, for its origin. Looking back on this adventure in 1979, McClintock recalled a dramatic scene that could have been written in Hollywood. In early 1957, maize geneticist Paul Christof Mangelsdorf had stopped by for a visit at McClintock's lab at Cold Spring Harbor, so she gave him a ride to the train station. As he left, he asked without preface, would she be willing to spend several weeks training technicians in Peru in the fine art of cytology? Known for her remarkable skill in preparing slides that captured the key moments in cell division, McClintock was a natural for the job. Without hesitation she agreed to it.

Not long after this encounter, McClintock received a formal invitation to join the "Races of Maize" project, which sought to trace the origins of maize, since it has no wild type. The project, directed by the Committee on Preservation of Indigenous Strains of Maize, was cosponsored by the National Academies of Science and the National Research Council (NAS-NRC) and largely funded by the Rockefeller Foundation.

In addition to McClintock's primary research, from 1957 to 1981 she was active in a Rockefeller Institution effort to trace the origins of maize, teaching her techniques to Latin American technicians and researchers who were pursuing the question in their respective countries. Here McClintock is working in the lab at Cold Spring Harbor in April 1963. (The Barbara McClintock Papers, American Philosophical Society)

At first glance, this line of research appears to reside far from her major interests, but McClintock found she could uncover the roots of this plant's ancestry through cytogenetic analysis and comparison of modern plants grown in different areas of Latin America. This work came to dovetail nicely with McClintock's interest in the evolution of maize. She spent about six weeks in the winter of 1957 in Molina and Lima, Peru, and after that a few weeks a year for 20 years in various Latin American countries, teaching cytological technique to Latin American researchers. From 1962 to 1964, she participated in a similar Rockefeller-funded program at North Carolina State College (now University) in Raleigh.

Reevaluation and Recognition

In the early 1950s, French biologist François Jacob and French biochemist Jacques Lucien Monod of the Pasteur Institute in Paris discovered a similar system of gene controllers, in bacteria, that they called the operon system, composed of a "regulator" and an "operator." In 1960, McClintock wrote up a comparison showing the parallels between their system and her own—but that also stirred up little interest. Even though she had sent Jacob and Monod a copy of her paper, they failed to mention her work in their landmark 1961 paper describing the operon system. When they came to Cold Spring Harbor for the annual symposium the following summer, however, they tried to patch up their gaffe with this statement:

> *Long before regulator and operator genes were revealed in bacteria, the extensive and penetrating work of McClintock*

> ... had revealed the existence, in maize, of two classes of
> genetic "controlling elements" whose specific mutual relation-
> ships are closely comparable with those of the regulator and
> the operator. . . .

This public statement marked the beginning of recognition in the genetics community that McClintock's work in this arena was far more generalized than most researchers thought. Along with their colleague, French microbiologist André Michel Lwoff, at the Pasteur Institute, Jacob and Monod won the 1965 Nobel Prize in physiology or medicine for this work.

Awards Abound in the 1960s and 1970s

By the 1960s and 1970s, a shower of awards began to celebrate McClintock's scientific prowess, although not for the jumping gene. She was considered brilliant without it, but, unfortunately, she was not well satisfied with the accolades: First, she was a private person and did not like being the center of attention, and second, she knew, or at least sensed, that her greatest contribution was her discovery of mobile elements.

In 1959, McClintock was elected to the National Academy of Arts and Sciences, and in 1967, she received the Kimber Medal from the National Academy of Sciences. In 1970, she became the first woman to receive the National Medal of Science, the highest government award in science. In 1973, Cold Spring Harbor Laboratory dedicated the McClintock Laboratory, and 1981 proved to be a star-studded year, as she received the MacArthur Prize Fellow Laureate Award (sometimes known as the "Genius Award") the Wolf Prize in Medicine, the Albert Lasker Basic Medical Research Award, and the Thomas Hunt Morgan Medal (shared with Marcus Rhoades).

When McClintock's old friend George Beadle heard about the Wolf Prize in Medicine, which she shared with Stanley Cohen, Beadle wrote to her: "That is great but as everyone knowledgeable of the situation agrees it should have been recognized long ago in your case. . . . I admit in the early stages of your most remarkable work I was skeptical," he continued, "but that was years ago." The greatest recognition, however, was yet to come.

The Nobel Prize

The date was October 10, 1983, and Barbara McClintock was listening to early morning radio in her apartment. Most Nobelists hear the good news from a phone call ringing in the middle of the night—at least that is frequently the case for Nobel laureates in the United States, since the call comes from Stockholm, Sweden. McClintock, however, lived so frugally that she did not even have a telephone at her apartment. That is why she first heard of the Nobel committee's decision on a radio news program. Her first reaction was a murmured complaint: "Oh, dear." She was no doubt thinking of the days of work she would miss and, well, all the unwanted personal attention (as opposed to attention to her work, which she valued). From childhood throughout her scientific career to the end of her life, she preferred to be in control. Winning the Nobel Prize tends to sweep one up in festivities and accolades. There would be the trip to Sweden, speeches to make, a banquet to attend—all unproductive from McClintock's point of view.

At 81, she still put in her usual schedule, starting with a brisk walk up the road in Cold Spring Harbor. She usually dressed in practical clothes—denim jeans, a no-frills tailored shirt, and sturdy walking shoes. On these walks, she typically trekked through the woods or down Bungtown Road to the Sand Spit and back. Along the way, she continually stopped to look at the plants growing along the roadside or scattered about the woods that she passed through. If a friend or student had come along, she might launch into a lecture about the flora they passed. McClintock never stopped working. She would notice patterns in the flowers or leaves that set her thinking about the genes that governed them, about control. She threw the large net of her mind over the diversity and patterns and integrated, as she liked to say of her thought processes. She would formulate the connections in heredity, development, and evolution. To her the walks were another perspective, another way of looking at her work. Sometimes she gathered walnuts along the way, as she did on this morning, the morning when she received the announcement of her Nobel Prize.

To McClintock, this was a morning in her life like any other, and she saw no reason to change her routine. When recognition and encouragement might have helped her through emotionally difficult times, she felt the scientific community had not understood and had left her solitary and doubted. She had made her way through those

In October 1983, Barbara McClintock was named sole Nobel laureate in physiology or medicine for that year. (The Barbara McClintock Papers, American Philosophical Society)

times by withdrawing into her work. Now, with all the accolades, she was not glad. As her friend Howard Green said in an article after her death, "Barbara rose to a stratospheric level in the general esteem of the scientific world and honors were showered upon her. But she could hardly bear them. She felt obliged to submit to them. It was not joy or even satisfaction that she experienced, it was martyrdom! To have her work understood and acknowledged was one thing, but to make public appearances and submit to ceremonies was quite another." News reporters spoke of her as "intensely private" and a "no-nonsense researcher," but she had an upside and always enjoyed a good joke. How much more might she have bloomed if the trust and encouragement had come earlier in her career? That, however, is not the way the cards were dealt.

Finally, she was ready. She knew what the world expected. "I knew I was going to be in for something," she noted. "I had to psych myself up. I had to think of the significance of it all; to react. I had to know what approach I would take." She told the lab administrative director she would do what she needed to do, following up with the obligatory press release and press conference. Her press release was upbeat, asserting that it seemed unfair "to reward a person for hav-ing so much pleasure, over the years, asking the maize plant to solve specific problems and then watching its responses."

For the press conference, McClintock perched on a stool, dressed in her regular uniform—freshly ironed denim pants and tailored shirt—her weather-beaten face brightened by piercing eyes and her short, brown hair slightly grayed. Surprised when a reporter told her the prize was worth around $190,000, her wide-eyed response filled the room with laughter, "Oh it is," she murmured. Later in the conference, she thanked the Carnegie Institution of Washington, expressing appreciation for the freedom she had to pursue the jump-ing gene despite its long-lived unpopularity among her colleagues. "The Carnegie Institution," she said, "never once told me that I shouldn't be doing it. They never once said I should publish when I wasn't publishing."

The reporters pressed the question. Had the long wait for this recognition made her bitter? She put on her public face and told the truth—or most of it. "No, no, no," she replied. This moment was not

Why Not Sooner?

When Barbara McClintock became a Nobel Laureate, James D. Watson remarked, in the role of director of the Cold Spring Harbor laboratories: "It is not a controversial award. No one thinks of genetics now without the implications of her work." The comment seems strangely defensive, but the Nobel committee often comes under criticism for its choices, and, as Watson knew well, Barbara McClintock's work had enjoyed, at best, mixed approbation since her 1951 symposium presentation.

Today, though, the question most asked is certainly not *why* she became a Nobel laureate but rather: What took so long? Watson himself and his colleague Francis H. C. Crick received their Nobel in 1962, nine years after their 1953 discovery of the structure of the DNA molecule. McClintock's work on mobile genetic elements dates back to 1944—with a Nobel award in 1983, nearly 40 years later. Scientists like to say that science is self-correcting, but sometimes it takes awhile. In the case of Barbara McClintock, acknowledgement of her discoveries and their importance was admittedly a long time coming.

Some people automatically point their fingers at facts like these and chalk up the discrepancy to gender discrimination, and, as already mentioned, McClintock did encounter some obstacles because of what she sometimes called the "anti-woman scientist bias." This time, though, the more likely explanation lay in the flow of contemporary discovery and understanding of the work's importance. Watson and Crick's insight into the structure of DNA, followed by Marshall W. Nirenberg, Robert W. Holley, and Har Gobine Khorana's deciphering of the genetic code in 1968, made the importance of the two discoveries perfectly obvious. Clearly, if any change occurred in a single nucleotide, that part of the genetic code would convey completely different hereditary information.

The scientific community was not so well prepared in the 1940s–50s for McClintock's concept of mobile genetic elements. Not only did the concept fly in the face of the still-accepted "pearls strung immutably on the chromosome" view of genes but also McClintock presented mobile elements in the context of maize, an organism that was relatively unfamiliar to much of the scientific community. Also, was the existence of mobile elements universal or was it restricted to the rather complex biology of the maize plant? Once other researchers found transposons in bacteria and insects, and then when transposition of growth regulatory genes were seen to be involved in cancer, the Nobel committee had a clear path to distinguish McClintock with an unshared award and did so in short order. As one reporter put it, "The world has finally begun to catch up to 'Barb' McClintock."

the time for complaints. "You're having a good time. You don't need public recognition. . . . When you know you're right you don't care. You can't be hurt. You just know, sooner or later, it will come out in the wash. . . ."

McClintock was living the life she had longed for as a young high school student in love with the process of finding out, with the joy inherent in the process of attaining knowledge, and now she took the opportunity to celebrate that lifestyle: "It's such a pleasure," she told the reporters, "to carry out an experiment when you think of something—carry it out and watch it go—it's a great, great pleasure. . . . I've had a very, very satisfying and interesting life."

The crowd of men and women in formal evening dress burst into thunderous applause when King Carl Gustaf of Sweden presented the Nobel award to McClintock. Her story had captured imaginations worldwide—a response to her commitment to excellence and perseverance in face of adversity and prejudice.

After the Nobel

In the years that surrounded the Nobel award, a growing appreciation built up for Barbara McClintock's extraordinary achievement displayed in a highly integrated body of work. With the discovery of the structure of DNA, the Nobel announcement asserted that McClintock's work was "one of the two great discoveries of our times in genetics." The award made McClintock the first American woman to receive an unshared Nobel, the seventh woman to receive a Nobel Prize in science, only the second recipient to have waited so long, and the first specializing in studies of large plant life. American evolutionary biologist Ernst Mayr offered this summary of McClintock's overall contribution in his book *The Growth of Biological Thought: Diversity, Evolution, and Inheritance* (1982): "Barbara McClintock used [the] attributes of maize during thirty years of brilliant studies for an interpretation of gene action, the comprehensiveness of which was not generally realized until the molecular geneticists, years later, arrived at similar conclusions."

In the wake of the Nobel Prize, many other honors were showered upon her, including induction into the National Women's Hall of Fame in 1986. None of them, however, was particularly welcomed by McClintock. Much of the attention centered on the fact that she was a woman. She was supportive of equal rights and job opportunities not only for women but also for other minorities such as African Americans and Jews, and she accepted her responsibility of being a role model—a living promise of possibilities for women. Much of this concept was positive, encouraging other women to broaden their ideas of what kinds of behavior are appropriate for women. Much of her success was based on traits that many people thought of as masculine: aggressively protecting her freedom; playing the role of eccentric maverick; operating comfortably with an objective, rather than subjective, worldview; looking at the big picture or, as people might say today, "thinking outside the box"; and, of course, wearing pants instead of dresses most of the time. However, people began to make claims about her that she did not embrace so enthusiastically. When Keller's biography, *A Feeling for the Organism,* came out in 1983, some of the author's phrases, such as references to McClintock's "intimate knowledge" or "a mystical understanding" of maize, attracted the attention of readers who were looking for a uniquely feminine form of science. While the biography is one of the strongest sources available on McClintock, it may have suffered from McClintock's apparent distancing from the project after five interviews. Seeing McClintock as a reclusive, brilliant mystic, Keller described a woman whose "passion is for the individual, for the difference." This focus on the particular attracted those who were put off by the objectivity of science and who favored Eastern thought over Western traditions of rational thinking and scientific method. McClintock, however, clearly sought to uncover generalized, broad, fundamental biological truths based on the exploration of evidence taken from the individual instances she studied—observing great biological principles such as evolution through the window provided by maize plants. A controversy ensued, with most of those who knew her well seeing neither the recluse nor the mystic that Keller seemed to see. McClintock did not consider herself a mystic, commenting that she neither accepted nor rejected what she did not understand, remarking, "You just don't know."

Following the Nobel announcement, McClintock felt overcome by invitations to speak, additional awards, requests for interviews, and other invasions of her privacy and work routine, and perhaps because of the overload of attention, when the book was published, she refused to read it, grumbling, "I want nothing to do with a book about me. I do not like publicity." As always, she preferred to forget about "the me." Nevertheless, the book enjoyed a wide readership and encouraged the growing interest in Barbara McClintock, her work, and how she fought for the right to pursue her interests.

The Last Years

When Maria Goeppert-Mayer received the 1963 Nobel Prize in physics, she remarked in an interview, "If you love science, all you really want is to keep on working. The Nobel prize thrills you, but it

McClintock remained active in her field and kept up with new discoveries being made throughout her later years—avidly participating at meetings. Here she is chatting with former CSHL director John Cairns in the late 1980s at a meeting on Eukaryotic Transposable Elements as Mutagenic Agents. (Cold Spring Harbor Laboratory Archives)

changes nothing." In Barbara McClintock's case, it did not matter at all. As much as possible, she just kept on working.

She continued her 12-hour workday into her late eighties, reducing her exercise regime to aerobic dance, only slightly less strenuous than the running she had always done. She read voraciously as always, conscientiously keeping up with advances in molecular biology and an encyclopedic array of other topics, her journals neatly stacked, filled with underlining and annotated in coded colors of ink.

For McClintock's 90th birthday, molecular biologist Nina V. Fedoroff (who had worked with McClintock on a molecular analysis of maize mobile elements) and other friends presented her with a volume of essays, *The Dynamic Genome,* in her honor. Just a small group of friends—most of them authors of the essays—gathered on the porch of James Watson's house to read what they had written, "reflecting," in Fedoroff's words, "the pursuits and passions ignited by the sparks and embers scattered from the fierce blaze of McClintock's intellect through the decades of this century of genetics."

As McClintock approached ninety, she told a caller, "I'm almost ninety, and in my family ninety is the end, and I'm beginning to feel it." She had begun to wind down, and on September 2, 1992, Barbara McClintock died near Cold Spring Harbor, in Huntington, New York. As she had predicted, she was 90 years old.

9

Barbara McClintock: Personal Integrity and Solid Science

Beneath the layers of Barbara McClintock's story lies a disturbing question: If McClintock was right in the insights she proposed about controlling elements in maize, was science wrong then? The answer is yes, scientists can be wrong. Often the best explanation that can be tested is almost right—and for the moment that may be the best anyone can do. As happened in the case of McClintock, sometimes some new facts are yet to be uncovered before a hypothesis can be fully tested. Sometimes, as McClintock's former student and colleague Harriet Creighton once said, you have to know the right questions to ask. Eventually, though, the right questions do get asked, new data come in, new tests and experiments are done—and science self-corrects. That is one of the beauties of science. With different researchers constantly nibbling away at the giant task of understanding our universe, science always self-corrects, eventually.

A Philosophy Made to Fit

Throughout her life, Barbara McClintock embraced independence and autonomy. From the undergraduate years at Cornell to the last days at Cold Spring Harbor, she decisively pursued a life unencumbered by commitments to family, friends, acquaintances, or scholastic administrators. Some women scientists of her time pursued both a family life and a career in science. In the previous generation, Marie Curie managed to "have it all," raising a daughter alone as what we would call today a "single mother" after the death of her husband Pierre. She may have had domestic help, but the responsibility was still hers. Barbara McClintock, however, apparently felt no need for such intimate relationships and interdependency, or if she did, she kept that part of her life private. Her mind worked differently. The only intimacy she seemed to need was the close and continuous companionship of her work. She was a good friend to those who understood her and spoke her language. But she owed no one and expected no special consideration. She only asked for recognition for the contributions she made to science. Otherwise, like Greta Garbo, as far as the public knows, she simply wished "to be left alone." She wished to explore what intrigued her, it seems, and pursue the puzzles that challenged her extraordinary analytical gifts.

Curie and McClintock, though different in their attitudes toward relationships, shared a dedication to science that emerged in the language they used to describe their lives. Curie often described the ascetic self-denial she endured for her work—the shortage of food and the frozen surface in the water bowl she used for washing. McClintock spoke of her incredible luck and her joy at discovery and her pleasure in solving problems. She loved her life—despite the difficult period of rejection and ostracism, which clearly was hurtful to her. Both women lived lives devoted to science and the quest for knowledge and both tried to communicate the measure of that devotion to the public.

Yet McClintock painted a picture of herself as a person without commitments, even the commitment to a career. She emphasized that she simply followed her interests. "There was no thought of a career, just enjoying myself immensely because what I was doing was so interesting." What she really did in this statement was to emphasize that her commitment was private. She had made a private, maybe even unconscious, promise to herself that she would always stay true to herself, that she would follow her dream, and she did. She let nothing else and no one else get in the way, and in every way that was open to her, she kept control of her own destiny.

McClintock had some difficult years, when her colleagues denied her a fair hearing and her research results were unpopular with her peers. She stood firm, however, and learned to work happily—even joyously—without the camaraderie she had enjoyed in the days of the cytology group at Cornell. She took advantage of her solitary privacy and focused ever more keenly on her work, always finding joy in solving the puzzles and exploring the new territory she discovered.

At one point in the 1980s, chatting with Harvard University biology students after a seminar she was teaching, McClintock advised them to "take the time and look" at every aspect of the organisms they studied, to seek out the complexities hidden in every system, to be able to know it through and through. The students saw her point, as did other biologists. Despite pressures created by new technology, tight schedules, and the "business" matters of funding and patents, the real work of biology requires abundant, thoughtful time for understanding. Only then does one gain the depth of comprehension that produces another level of thought processes. Only then does one gain a truly productive mind-set that allows the mental tools of integration and synthesis to do their work.

Spanning the Century

During her lifetime of sustained work in cytogenetics, McClintock spanned nearly a century of dramatic changes in the scientific study of the biological world. A classicist in technique and a devotee of maize as a tool for studying genetics, McClintock became tagged by many molecular geneticists as outside the mainstream. When she talked about maize, she was speaking a different language—an out-of-date language, they thought. By then, molecular biology and microbiology had moved to the cutting edge of research. The study of bacteria offered much higher generation rates—*E. coli,* for example, reproduces at a rate of about 50 generations per day, or about 15,000 per year—offering results at a staggeringly faster rate than maize or even fruit flies. However, after awhile, as the *Time* magazine reporter wrote, they began to "catch up" with her. She had been talking the same language after all, the language of all living things—not just maize. As Jacques Lucien Monod and François Jacob discovered in the 1960s, her transposable element was a close relative of the operon system they found in bacteria as she pointed out in her 1960 paper. This recognition showed that jumping genes were not just an oddity of maize, and today transposons are recognized as a universal phenomenon. In fact, researchers can detect transposition more easily in bacterial transposons because they can work with large populations, enabling them to test more easily for particular characteristics.

By the time the Nobel committee announced McClintock's award in 1983, many of her colleagues had come to appreciate her commitment to science—not as a "career," not as an avenue to discovery for the fame and fortune of being first, but for the beauty of finding new information and integrating new facts into the constantly changing scientific worldview.

Today McClintock's work on mobile elements has gained recognition for its insights into the chromosome's processes when breakage and mending occur—insights that have led to important breakthroughs in the techniques of genetic engineering and the understanding of disease. For example, according to molecular biologist Nina Fedoroff, Pennsylvania State University still has maize transposable elements that were cloned in its laboratory almost 20 years ago and are now widely used for insertional mutagenesis—the generation of mutation using insertion techniques.

"Jumping genes" have also helped biologists understand how bacteria are able to develop resistance to many different antibiotics and also how jumping genes may facilitate the transformation of normal cells to cancerous cells.

"I've Had Such a Good Time. . . ."

In 2005, the United States Postal Service released a Barbara McClintock postage stamp, one of a set of stamps commemorating great American scientists of the 20th century. In the artfully displayed portrait and maize plant, her sparkling eyes, crooked smile, and weather-beaten face shine out like the image of a kindly grandmother—definitely a woman capable of joy. Many people react to McClintock's story as a saga of a lonely figure, a victim of discrimination, but she never allowed this view of herself. She was a solitary person, living in the world of her work, but she was not lonely. This was a woman who once said of her college dates, "These attachments wouldn't have lasted. I was just not adjusted, never had been, to being closely associated with anybody, even members of my own family." These are not the words of a person who regrets her years of living alone. Being alone gave her time to think. McClintock was also the object of discrimination, as were her female colleagues, but she did not look at herself as a victim.

The loyalty of her friends and the respect that finally came her way speak of a unique and independent woman whose work called to her with a power that could not be denied. As McClintock remarked to reporters at the Cold Spring Harbor press conference in 1983, "I've had such a good time. I can't imagine having a better one. No, no that's true. I've had a very, very satisfactory and interesting life."

Among her friends, McClintock was known as extraordinary, gifted with a great intellectual capacity. She spoke bluntly and directly, and she expected those around her to do the same, moving along at the same pace and taking advantage of what she had to offer. As her friend Henry Green wrote, "There has never been anyone like Barbara McClintock in this world, nor ever will be." Named by James Watson as one of the 20th century's greatest figures in genetics, Barbara McClintock was, in the words of Marcus Rhoades, "one of the intellectual giants of her time."

CHRONOLOGY

1902	Barbara McClintock is born on June 16 in Hartford, Connecticut.
1908	The McClintock family moves to Brooklyn, New York.
1915	Thomas Hunt Morgan publishes his chromosome theory of heredity, first proposed in 1902.
1916–19	McClintock attends Erasmus Hall High School.
1919	Enrolls in the College of Agriculture at Cornell University in Ithaca, New York
1923	Receives a bachelor's degree from Cornell University
1925	Receives a master's degree from Cornell University
1927	Receives a doctorate degree from Cornell University
1927–31	Joins the Cornell University faculty as instructor of botany
1929	First major publication, sole author: "Chromosome morphology in *Zea mays.*" *Science* 69: 629
1931	With Harriet Creighton, publishes in the August 7 *Proceedings of the National Academy of Sciences,* proving that during meiosis genetic material crosses over from one chromosome to its pair

1931–33   Receives a two-year fellowship from the National
                   Research Council

                   Reports on ring chromosomes (though not the first
                   to do so) and names the nucleolar organizer region
                   (NOR)

1933–34   Receives a fellowship from the Guggenheim
                   Foundation for study in Germany, returning early
                   because of the country's political unrest

1934–36   Serves as research associate at Cornell University
                   on a fellowship from the Rockefeller Foundation

1936–42   Joins the University of Missouri faculty as assistant
                   professor of botany, working with Lewis Stadler on
                   the effects of X-rays on chromosomes

1938   Names the breakage-fusion-bridge cycle

1939   Elected vice president of the Genetics Society of
                   America

1943   Becomes a permanent staff member at the Carnegie
                   Institution of Washington's Department of Genetics
                   at Cold Spring Harbor, New York

1944   Works on *Neurospora* (red bread mold), identifying
                   its seven chromosomes

1944   Elected to membership in the National Academy
                   of Sciences (the third woman to receive this
                   honor)

1945   Elected president of the Genetics Society of
                   America (the first woman in that office)

1946   Elected member of the American Philosophical
                   Society

1947	Receives Achievement Award from the Educational Foundation of the American Association of University Women
1951	Presents paper on transposable elements (dubbed "jumping genes" by reporters) at an unenthusiastic Cold Spring Harbor meeting
1953	Publishes a second paper on transposons
1953	James Watson and Francis Crick announce their breakthrough discovery of the double-helix structure of DNA, resulting in increased focus on the new science of molecular biology.
1956	McClintock presents another paper on transposons at Cold Spring Harbor.
1957–59	Trains geneticists in Latin America in cytological methods for tracing the origins of maize (Rockefeller Foundation Agricultural Program)
1959	Elected member of the American Academy of Arts and Science
1963–81	Becomes further involved in tracing the evolution of maize and in training Latin American geneticists at North Carolina State University
1965	Named Andrew D. White Professor at Large at Cornell University
1967–92	Becomes Distinguished Service Member of the Carnegie Institution of Washington Department of Genetics at Cold Spring Harbor
1967	Receives the Kimber Genetics Award from the National Academy of Sciences

1970   Awarded the National Medal of Science (the first woman recipient)

1973   Dedication of McClintock Laboratory at Cold Spring Harbor Laboratory

1980   Links her work to bacterial transposons

1981   Receives the MacArthur Prize Fellow Laureate Award, the Wolf Prize in Medicine, the Albert Lasker Basic Medical Research Award, and the Thomas Hunt Morgan Medal (shared with Marcus Rhoades)

1983   Receives the Nobel Prize in physiology or medicine (sole recipient)

1987   *The Discovery and Characterization of Transposable Elements: The Collected Papers of Barbara McClintock* is published.

1992   Barbara McClintock dies at the age of 90 on September 2 in Huntington, New York.

2003   Completion of the human genome (the complete genetic code of humans) project, providing geneticists with a map that shows the location of every gene in the human body

allele   an alternative form of a gene positioned in the same place on its counterpart or partner chromosome and controlling the same characteristic

botany   the study of plants, their structure and processes (botanist: a plant biologist)

cell   the basic unit for living organisms

centromere   during cell division, the point where two chromatids, or chromosome strands, remain attached to each other and also attach to the spindle

chiasma (plural: chiasmata)   point where parts of a chromosome visually appear to cross

chromatid   during cell division, one of the two strands of a chromosome after it has replicated lengthwise

chromosome   the rod-shaped structure in a cell nucleus that carries GENES, which control what traits are expressed by an organism; genes are inherited on chromosomes, i.e., they are passed on from one generation to another on chromosomes

cotyledon   the first embryonic plant leaf to appear from a sprouting seed

crossing over   during meiosis, when replicated chromosomes line up to form pairs, one inherited from each parent, they separate partially, joined at the CHIASMATA; at that location, crossing over (the exchange of CHROMATIDS) may take place

cytogenetics   the combined study of genetics and cytology, the structure of cells

cytology   the study of a cell's structure and processes

diploid   having a set of paired chromosomes in each nucleus—and therefore twice the haploid number of chromosomes

DNA (deoxyribonucleic acid)   at the molecular level, the chemical (specifically, a nucleic acid) that carries genetic information; chromosomes are composed primarily of DNA

dominant trait   describes a gene that controls the appearance of a characteristic in a parent and also causes the characteristic to appear the same in the offspring as in the parent; also used to describe the characteristic produced by a dominant gene (see RECESSIVE)

empirical   based on observation, experiment, and experience

endosperm   in many seed plants, seed tissue that provides food for the embryo

enzyme   specialized proteins that control the speed of biochemical reactions

gamete   a special cell (for example, an ovum, or egg cell, or a sperm cell) containing a single (haploid) complement of chromosomes instead of a full double complement; also known as a "sex cell." In maize, meiosis produces spores (megaspores and microspores [sporogenesis]), which then undergo mitosis to produce gametes

gene   (from the Greek word meaning "to give birth to") the name given by botanist Wilhelm Johanssen in 1909 to the small carriers, or units, of hereditary information, which in turn are located on chromosomes within the nucleus of a cell

genetics   the branch of biology that focuses on heredity and the study of its agents, such as the gene and the chromosome, and processes that effect variations in traits that are passed from generation to generation of an organism

genome   the full set of genetic information found on the chromosomes (and the genes they carry) for a given species and inherited by the individual organism from its parents

haploid   having a single set of unpaired chromosomes in each nucleus

heredity   the passing on of genetically controlled traits from one generation to the next

homologous   similar, having the same function or structure; one of a pair but not entirely identical, for example, a homologous chromosome

hybrid   a plant produced by a cross between two plants or animals having a differing but similar genetic makeup, such as two different but similar species (such as a donkey and a horse to produce a hybrid mule) or varieties of the same species

hypothesis   a statement set forth as a basis for further investigation and testing; potential predecessor to a THEORY

"jumping gene"   name given to TRANSPOSON by news reporters

linkage   association of two or more genes located near each other on a chromosome and therefore often inherited together

maize   Indian corn, having colorful kernel patterns

meiosis   a process of cell division that takes place in organisms (including plants) that reproduce sexually; the parent cell's nucleus divides into four nuclei, each containing half the usual number of chromosomes (compare mitosis); other names for these daughter cells: GAMETES, sex cells, or germ cells in many lifeforms, but in maize, meiosis produces spores, which then undergo mitosis to produce sex cells (also true of other organisms with an alternation of generations)

Mendelism   the scientific study of genetics and inheritance based on breeding experiments and the formulation of governing laws first set out by Gregor Mendel

mitosis   a process of cell division that forms two daughter cells having the same number of chromosomes as the parent cell (see MEIOSIS)

morphological   structural, for example, the tassel is a morphological feature of maize; a knob on a chromosome is a morphological genetic feature

mutation   a random change in a parent gene or chromosome (caused, for example, by exposure to X-rays), which may be inherited by offspring and expressed as a changed trait or characteristic

nucleolar organizer region (NOR)   a small structure that must be present in a cell for a proper nucleolus to be formed

nucleolus   a small, spherical body found inside a cell nucleus, the production site for fundamental structural elements of ribosomes (protein "factories")

recessive   describes a gene that only produces an effect in offspring when the matching allele is identical; also used to describe the characteristic produced by a recessive gene (see DOMINANT)

ring chromosome   a broken chromosome that has formed a ring by joining its two ends

spindle   a football-shaped structure with drawn-out fibers that radiate from one side of the cell to the other; during meiosis and mitosis, chromosomes lengthen and are distributed along these fibers

theory   a naturalistic explanation of facts that has been thoroughly and objectively tested by many experimenters

trait   (in genetics) a quality or characteristic that is controlled by one or more genes, for example, tallness or leaf color

transposable element sometimes referred to as a "jumping gene," a segment of DNA that can change its position on a chromosome or move (transpose) to another chromosome, thereby often influencing the action of nearby genes; called transposons in bacteria

transposon a transposable element containing bacterial genes; also sometimes synonymous with TRANSPOSABLE ELEMENT

FURTHER READING

Books

Adler, Robert E. "McClintock's Chromosomes." *Science Firsts: From the Creation of Science to the Science of Creation*, 162–167. Hoboken, N.J.: John Wiley & Sons, 2002.

> *This book of 35 profiles of scientists on the cutting edge includes a succinct and informative chapter on Barbara McClintock, offering insights to her stature and her scientific contributions from a 21st-century perspective.*

Andreasen, Nancy C. *The Creating Brain: The Neuroscience of Genius.* New York: Dana Press, 2005.

> *This highly recommended book sounds difficult but is accessible and filled with many fascinating and memorable examples of genius at work and the nature of genius, from Mozart to Einstein. Nancy Andreasen points out that our society is not supportive of genius and often does not even recognize it. She hopes to encourage budding genius and an appreciation of genius both for extraordinary young people and for the further enrichment of humanity by their works. Andreasen has mined her dual academic background for this book: the humanities (Ph.D. in Renaissance literature) and psychiatry (an M.D. specializing in psychiatry). She is the Andrew H. Woods Chair of Psychiatry and director of the Mental Health Clinical Research Center at the University of Iowa Carver College of Medicine, as well as editor of the American Journal of Psychiatry).*

Comfort, Nathaniel C. *The Tangled Field: Barbara McClintock's Search for the Patterns of Genetic Control.* Cambridge, Mass.: Harvard University Press, 2003.

> *Comfort's biography explores McClintock's work in detail, at the same time offering a thoughtful discussion of her struggles to protect her independence, her right to pursue fruitful research, and her effort to make herself heard.*

Dash, Joan. *The Triumph of Discovery: Women Scientists Who Won the Nobel Prize.* Englewood Cliffs, N.J.: Julian Messner, 1991.

> *Short, easy-to-read biographical entries.*

Fine, Edith H. *Barbara McClintock: Nobel Prize Geneticist.* Berkeley Heights, N.J.: Enslow Publishers, 1998.

> *Fine talks about her writing with joy, and she has a knack for putting life into every page. Her book is nearly 10 years old, but it is still a good source.*

Hine, Robert, ed. *The Facts On File Dictionary of Biology.* 4th ed. New York: Facts On File, 2005.

> *Recently updated, this resource contains succinct, well-researched entries defining basic biological principles, concepts, and terms.*

Keller, Evelyn Fox. *A Feeling for the Organism: The Life and Work of Barbara McClintock.* New York: W. H. Freeman, 1983.

> *Published the year Barbara McClintock received her Nobel Prize, this lively, personal account is based on interviews with McClintock, her family, and her colleagues. The reader learns a lot about McClintock, her self-image, and her work, but of course does not gain the perspective of the passage of time.*

"McClintock, Barbara." *Current Biography Yearbook 1984.* New York: H. W. Wilson, 1984.

> *Brief biographical data.*

McGrayne, Sharon Bertsch. *Nobel Prize Women in Science: Their Lives, Struggles and Momentous Discoveries.* Rev. ed. Secaucus, N.J.: Carol Publishing Group, 1998.

> *This book offers excellent insights both into the development of the woman scientist in the 20th century and the fascinating work of the group of Nobel scientists who happened to be women. Each scientist profiled is the subject of a full chapter.*

Pasachoff, Naomi. *Barbara McClintock: Genius of Genetics.* Great Minds of Science. Berkeley Heights, N.J.: Enslow Publishers, Inc., 2006.

> *Written for middle school readers, this lively, easy-to-read, and carefully researched book is both engaging and packed with information.*

Yount, Lisa. *A to Z of Women in Science and Math.* New York: Facts On File, 1999.

Short biographical sketches of women scientists and mathematicians, from the earliest known to the present. Easy to read, informative, and well researched.

Barbara McClintock and the History of Science

This cluster of work represents some of the increasing interest over the last 10 years in Barbara McClintock and the true nature of her life and work. The "Perspectives" articles listed below are especially intended for reading by high school, college-age, and older readers. Energetic and critical, researchers such as Lee B. Kass, Christophe Bonneuil, and others have tried to do away with bias by seeking out documents to shed light on the muddled facts. They try to dig beneath the surface, using newly available correspondence and tapes that were previously restricted.

The following journal articles, abstracts, presentations, and book chapters give readers a sense of what these investigators are finding out. A good place to begin would be the following three articles: "Records and Recollections," by Lee B. Kass (2001); "Cornfests, Cornfabs and Cooperation: The Origins and Beginnings of the Maize Genetics Cooperation News Letter," by Kass, Christophe Bonneuil, and Edward K. Coe, Jr. (2005); and "Proof of Physical Exchange of Genes on the Chromosomes," by Coe and Kass (2005), providing a historical perspective on Creighton and McClintock's landmark study, published in 1931.

Bonneuil, Christophe, and Lee B. Kass. "Mapping and Seeing: Barbara McClintock and the Articulation of Genetics and Cytology in Maize Genetics, 1928–1935." Paper presented in March 2001 to a workshop on "The Mapping Cultures of 20th Century Genetics" at The Max Planck Institute for the History of Science, Berlin.

Coe, Edward K., Jr., and Lee B. Kass. "Proof of Physical Exchange of Genes on the Chromosomes." *Proceedings of the National Academy of Science* 102, no. 19 (May 2005): 6,641–6,656. Available online. URL: http://www.pnas.org/cgi/content/abstract/0407340102v1. Accessed on June 6, 2007. The authors review the data surrounding the publication of the Creighton and McClintock paper of 1931, offering a perspective on the continuing significance of Creighton and McClintock's findings more than 70 years later.

Kass, Lee B. "Harriet Creighton: Proud Botanist." *Plant Science Bulletin* 51(4): 118–125. Available online: URL: http://www.botany.org/ PlantScienceBulletin/PSB–2005–51–4.php#HARRIET. Accessed on June 6, 2007. Sprightly celebration of McClintock's perhaps best-known student, based on personal interviews given by Creighton to the author.

———. "Missouri Compromise: Tenure or Freedom? New Evidence Clarifies Why Barbara McClintock Left Academe." *Maize Genetics Cooperation Newsletter* 79 (April 2005): 52–71. Available online. URL: http://www.agron.missouri.edu/mnl/79/05kass.htm. Accessed on June 6, 2007. Although this article includes neither footnotes nor photographs, careful research with primary documents leads to new insights of McClintock's falling out with the University of Missouri, Columbia.

———. "Identification of Photographs for the Barbara McClintock Papers on the National Library of Medicine Website." *Maize Genetics Cooperation Newsletter* 78: 24–26. Available online. URL: http://www. agron.missouri.edu/mnl/78/04kass.html. Accessed on June 6, 2007. The author tells how access to primary documents, including recorded interviews and photos, has helped her in sleuthing out the identities of some otherwise unidentified or wrongly identified colleagues and acquaintances of McClintock's.

———. "Records and Recollections: A New Look at Barbara McClintock, Nobel Prize-Winning Geneticist." *Genetics* 164 (August 2003): 1,251–1,260. A fine article that uses actual records and documents to present a more accurate historical perspective of this scientist.

———. "Barbara McClintock: Botanist, cytologist, geneticist." *American Journal of Botany* 87, no. 6: 64. Available online. URL: http://www. ou.edu/cas/botanymicro/botany2000/sympos4/abstracts/1.shtml Accessed on June 6, 2007. An abstract of a presentation made at a symposium titled "Botany in the Age of Mendel" (Abstract #193).

———. "McClintock, Barbara, American Botanical Geneticist, 1902–1992." In *Plant Sciences,* edited by Richard Robinson. Farmington Hills, Mich.: Macmillan Science Library, USA, 2000. A clear, well-organized biographical sketch that illustrates McClintock's contribution to the field of genetics.

———, and Christophe Bonneuil. "Mapping and Seeing: Barbara McClintock and the Linking of Genetics and Cytology in Maize Genetics, 1928–1935," in *Classical Genetic Research and Its Legacy:*

The Mapping Cultures of 20th Century Genetics, edited by Hans-Jörg Rheinberger and Jean-Paul Gaudillière, 91–118. London: Routledge, 2004. Incisive chapter on McClintock's contributions to the development of mapping technologies as a classical geneticist.

———, Christophe Bonneuil, and Edward K. Coe, Jr. "Cornfests, Cornfabs and Cooperation: The Origins and Beginnings of the Maize Genetics Cooperation News Letter." *Genetics* 169 (April): 1,787–1,797. Available online. URL: http://www.genetics.org/cgi/content/full/169/4/1787. Accessed on June 6, 2007. Explores how Cornell's Rollins A. Emerson built productive networking among maize geneticists worldwide through open sharing of unpublished work.

———, and K. Gale. "McClintock, Barbara," In *Encyclopedia of Women in World History,* edited by Bonnie Smith, xx. New York: Oxford University Press, in press for November 2007.

Internet Resources

ASU Ask a Biologist. Arizona State University. Available online: URL: http://askabiologist.asu.edu. Modified June 16, 2006.

> *Designed for secondary school students, teachers, and parents, this site enables users to pose biology questions to Arizona State University faculty members.*

Profiles in Science: Barbara McClintock Papers. National Library of Medicine. Available online: URL: http://profiles.nlm.nih.gov/LL. Accessed June 16, 2006.

> *Made available through the combined efforts of the American Philosophical Society and the National Library of Medicine, this site provides an excellent biographical overview of McClintock's life, as well as selected digitized photographs and papers.*

A CHRONOLOGICAL SELECTION OF BARBARA McCLINTOCK'S KEY PAPERS

....

1929

"Chromosome morphology in *Zea mays*." *Science* 69: 629.

1931

"The order of the genes C, Sh, and Wx in *Zea mays* with reference to a cytologically known point in the chromosome." *Proceedings of the National Academy of Sciences* 17 (8): 485–491.

Creighton, Harriet B., and Barbara McClintock. "A correlation of cytological and genetical cross-ing-over in *Zea mays*." *Proceedings of the National Academy of Sciences* 17: 492–497.

(This and the preceding article, by McClintock, were published together as a combined reprint because the two complement each other and were intended to be read together.)

"Cytological observations of deficiencies involv-ing known genes, translocations and an inversion in *Zea mays*." *Missouri Agricultural Experiment Station Research Bulletin* 163: 1–30.

1932

"A correlation of ring-shaped chromosomes with variegation in *Zea mays*." *Proceedings of the National Academy of Science* 18: 677–681.

1933   "The association of non-homologous parts of chromosomes in the mid-prophase of meiosis in *Zea mays*." *Zeitschrift fur Zellforschung und mikroskopische Anatomie* 19: 191–237.

1934   "The relation of a particular chromosomal element to the development of the nucleoli in *Zea mays*." *Zeitschrift fur Zellforschung und mikroskopische Anatomie* 21: 294–328.

1938   "The fusion of broken ends of sister half-chromatids following chromatid breakage at meiotic anaphases." *Missouri Agricultural Experiment Station Research Bulletin* 290: 1–48.

1939   "The behavior in successive nuclear divisions of a chromosome broken at meiosis." *Proceedings of the National Academy of Science* 25: 405–416.

1941   "The association of mutants with homozygous deficiencies in *Zea mays*." *Genetics* 26: 542–571.

1941   "The stability of broken ends of chromosomes in *Zea mays*." *Genetics* 26: 234–282.

1942   "The fusion of broken ends of chromosomes following nuclear fusion." *Proceedings of the National Academy of Science* 11: 458–463.

1942   "Maize genetics." *Carnegie Institution of Washington Year Book* 41: 181–186.

1943   "Maize genetics." *Carnegie Institution of Washington Year Book* 42: 148–152.

1945   "Cytogenetic studies of maize and *Neurospora*." *Carnegie Institution of Washington Year Book* 44: 108–112.

1946   "Maize genetics." *Carnegie Institution of Washington Year Book* 45: 176–186.

1947   "Cytogenetic studies of maize and *Neurospora.*" *Carnegie Institution of Washington Year Book* 46: 146–152.

1948   "Mutable loci in maize." *Carnegie Institution of Washington Year Book* 47: 155–169.

1949   "Mutable loci in maize." *Carnegie Institution of Washington Year Book* 48: 142–154.

1951   "Chromosome organization and genic expression." *Cold Spring Harbor Symposium on Quantitative Biology* 16: 13–47.

1951   "Mutable loci in maize." *Carnegie Institution of Washington Year Book* 50: 174–181.

1957   "Controlling elements and the gene." In *Genetic Mechanisms: Structure and Function, Cold Spring Harbor Symposia on Quantitative Biology,* Volume 21 (4–12 June 1956): 197–216. The Biological Laboratory, Cold Spring Harbor, Long Island, New York. (Sometimes called McClintock 1956 because she gave the presentation in 1956.)

1961   "Some parallels between gene control systems in maize and in bacteria." *American Naturalist* 95, no. 884 (September–October 1961): 265–277.

INDEX